Edward Cline

FROM THE CROW'S NEST

I0429431

A Miscellany of Observations

Patrick Henry Press

FROM THE CROW'S NEST: Copyright © 2014 by Edward Cline. All rights reserved. No part of this book may be reproduced, transmitted or stored by any means without written permission of the author except in the case of brief quotations embodied in critical articles or reviews.

Library of Congress Cataloguing-in-Publication Data

Edward Cline (1946 -)
From the Crow's Nest: A Miscellany of Observations /Edward Cline

ISBN-13: 978-1499690620
ISBN-10: 1499690622

Patrick Henry Press, Williamsburg, Virginia

Back Cover: Portrait of the author by Roxanne Albertoli

Publisher's Note: This book is a collection of essays and commentaries originally published on Rule of Reason, blog site for the Center for the Advancement of Capitalism, and in other venues. They are copyrighted by the author.

Table of Contents

Foreword

Foreword

From the "crow's nest" of my own ship of life – not for me a comfortable billet below decks, snoozing with others in our swaying hammocks – I gain a long-range perspective on what is before me, around and below me, and what is on the horizon.

This is the sixth anthology of commentaries and essays collected from Rule of Reason and other weblogs over the years. They focus on current politics, Islam, freedom of speech, various cultural issues, and miscellaneous subjects. The startling and unexpected reelection of Barack Obama in 2012, in spite of all the evidence of all his policy failures, abuses of executive power, and threats and tantrums, for another four years – against all reason – to continue what frankly should be deemed a nihilist campaign to "deconstruct" America, should cause anyone who values his freedom and his life to enter into a state of permanent trepidation.

For a while, I had contemplated titling this volume *There is only the fight to recover what has been lost...,"* cadging a line from T.S. Eliot' s 1940 poem *Four Quartets*. The sentiment would have been appropriate, because most of the articles here are about what has been lost or demolished in contemporary politics and culture. But, I too much associated that line with that political harridan, Hillary D. Rodham (Clinton), and her 1969 Wellesley College senior thesis, "There is Only the Fight...: An Analysis of the Alinsky Model."

She quoted the line at the end of a long chunk of Eliot's poem, "East Coker," which I have read and was consequently depressed by its intrinsic and gloomy determinism. Her thesis is an encomium of Saul Alinsky, the Chicago theoretician and socialist political strategist and advocate of "community organizing."

Unfortunately, Clinton, Alinsky, and Eliot were too intimately linked in my mind to everything I detest in "practical politics," so I chucked the idea of appropriating the line for myself. What has been "lost" has been a great portion of our freedom under the weight of the Progressive welfare and security state.

Long Live Lady Liberty.

Edward Cline
Williamsburg, Virginia
June 2014

Freedom of Speech

Shutting Us Up For Our Own Good

You can't claim that liberals and other statists aren't industrious. They are tirelessly diligent in their quest to find more ways to infringe upon or abridge our freedoms.

Many of our freedoms are embodied in the Bill of Rights, and have been regularly targeted for amendment or excision, from gun ownership, to freedom of assembly (or association), to freedom of speech *vis-à-vis* criticizing Islam and campaign finance law restrictions. No right today is sacrosanct or beyond the government's wish to curtail or abolish.

Only just recently, Senate Majority Leader Harry Reid (D-NV), in the wake of his defeat at the Cliven Bundy Ranch in Nevada, introduced a bill to abridge political speech. Breitbart's Big Government reported on May 18th:

> On May 15, Senate Majority Leader Harry Reid (D-NV) announced the Senate Judiciary Committee will hold a hearing on June 3 on amending the U.S. Constitution to limit political speech. If ultimately adopted, it would mark the first time in American history that a constitutional amendment rescinded a freedom listed as among the fundamental rights of the American people.

The proposed amendment was introduced by Sen. Tom Udall (D-CO) as S.J.R. 19 and if ratified would become the Twenty-Eighth Amendment. It provides in part that "Congress shall have power to regulate the raising and spending of money and in-kind equivalents with respect [to] the Federal elections ... [and] State elections." The proposed amendment includes a provision that "Nothing in this article shall be construed to grant Congress the power to abridge the freedom of the press." So Breitbart News, *The New York Times*, and the mainstream media would be able to say whatever they want, but citizens and citizen groups such as the National Rifle Association could not.

It seems like Harry Reid and his cronies have been reading retired Supreme Court Justice John Paul Stevens's book, *Six Amendments: How and Why We Should Change the Constitution,* which I reviewed in "Justice Stevens's Liberty-Destroying Amendments," in three parts, the relevant Part here. Stevens recommended adding another amendment that would accomplish Reid's purposes and vitiate any freedom of speech protections. I wrote:

Stevens writes that there is nothing to fear from his proposed amendment:

> "A constitutional amendment authorizing Congress and the states to place "reasonable" limitations on campaign expenditures would allow corporations to make public announcements of their views but would prohibit them from engaging in the kind of repetitive and excessive advocacy that the candidates typically employ. It would also repudiate both the holding and the reasoning in the *Citizens United* case, giving corporations an unlimited right to spend their shareholders' money in election campaigns." (p. 78)

Do the shareholders want a corporation to spend their money advocating issues? To Stevens, their wishes are irrelevant. Do individuals who encounter "repetitive and excessive" advocacy mind such encounters? That's irrelevant, too. Of course, those on the opposite side of an issue might mind it, but, like Muslims who object to critical things being said and written about Islam, they can just ignore it. Speech, written, oral, or visually, after all, is not a form of physical aggression or force. But Stevens doesn't want the champions of big government and incremental socialism to be subjected to limitations on "hate speech" that he wishes to impose on financed counter-arguments. Democrats should be free to repeat their "excessive" and "repetitive" messages over and over again. It's the other guy who must be shut up. Stevens's suggested amendment, which requires force or the threat of force, reads:

> "Neither the First Amendment nor any other provision of this Constitution shall be construed to prohibit the Congress or any state from imposing reasonable limits on the amount of money that candidates for public office, or their supporters, may spend in election campaigns." (p. 79)

The second half of Reid's proposed amendment to the First Amendment is virtually identical in wording to Stevens's proposed new amendment.

Who will define what is "reasonable" and what is not? Is there an infallible mathematical formula that would define "reasonableness"? It would be okay, by Stevens, to abridge the scope of the First Amendment and thus eviscerate its essential, fundamental meaning, just a little bit, to silence those wealthy, anti-big-government people. vitiate.

How was Reid's proposed gutting of the First Amendment received by the press? With an obfuscating sigh of relief. Greg Sargent of The Washington Post, in his May 15th article, "Reid calls for constitutional amendment on campaign cash," selectively omits mentioning that the Democrats are as guilty of all the charges that Reid levies against the Republicans, that "money is speech and speech is money," that freshets of special interest money "flood our democracy," that only "billionaire oil barons" will initiate a "hostile takeover" of the country. One must ask oneself what level of depraved repression would lead an alleged "journalist" to handily forget which political party has made corruption, election rigging, and living the high life on other people's money a time-honored tradition – a party that has more wealthy donors and supporters than the Republican Party ever had.

Also, according to Reid and accepted uncritically by Sargent (and most liberals):

> The argument is that electing Republican lawmakers would do nothing to change this economic status quo, because the GOP continues to be organized around the

protection of the interests of their very wealthy backers, whose influence over the process must be broken before any serious policy response to inequality and stalled economic opportunity and mobility can happen.

After all, that recently-revealed Americans for Prosperity memo spelled out that the real goal of all those millions in anti-Obamacare ads is to persuade swing voters that the answer to their economic problems is as little government as possible. As the New York Times detailed recently, this vision of what is good for America would also benefit the Koch brothers' bottom line to an untold degree. Reid will reference that memo today.

I guess Democrats have no "very wealthy backs," neither in Hollywood, nor in the tech industry, nor in the insurance industry, nor on Wall Street. However, Nicole Flatow of the George Soros-funded Think Progress in her May 15th article, "Why the Senate's Top Leader Came Out for a Constitutional Amendment to Reverse *Citizens United*," confirmed the link between the wording of Reid's proposed amendment and Justice John Paul Stevens's proposed new amendment, and also the collusion between the two men.

Reid told BuzzFeed that former U.S. Supreme Court Justice John Paul Stevens persuaded him to join the effort, after Stevens called for the amendment earlier this year in his new book. Reid, who decides what votes get called as majority leader, said he will now hold hearings on the amendment proposed by Sen. Udall, as well as call a vote on the House floor.

Reid has not been alone in proposing to gag corporations and non-Democratic non-profits over the amounts of money they spend on issues during election periods. Flatow wrote:

Since 2010, movements to pass a constitutional amendment overturning the U.S. Supreme Court's decision in *Citizens United v. FEC* have gained significant ground, with a number of states passing resolutions calling for a constitutional amendment. As one California legislator put it who introduced the bill that passed his state: "No one is

4.

underestimating how difficult it is, and justifiably so, to amend the Constitution. But being silent is worse." And a number of top Democratic senators have proposed amendments in Congress for several years now, including Tom Udall (NM), Michael Bennett (CO), Tom Harkin (IA), Dick Durbin (IL), Chuck Schumer (NY), Sheldon Whitehouse (RI), and Jeff Merkely (OR).

Many of the usual suspects., *non sunt?*

To Democrats and other power-lusting politicians, the Constitution has served as an impediment to "real social change." And that Constitutional requirement of needing either two-thirds of both houses of Congress, or passage by legislatures in three-fourths of states, to enact an amendment, is just another disdained, antiquated obstacle to "voicing the people's will" and empowering the democratic mobs controlled and manipulated by the Democrats.

The premier opponent of those Constitutional impediments – at least, the one in the brightest limelight – is President Barack Obama. He, Reid, and all the other suspects are on the same page. Paul Roderick Gregory in his September 23rd, 2012 Forbes article, "Why The Fuss? Obama Has Long Been On Record In Favor of Redistribution":

> In 2001, then state senator and University of Chicago law lecturer, Barack Obama, sat down for a public radio interview. At the time, he did not anticipate a near-term run for the presidency. He spoke candidly and deliberately about how to "break free" of Constitutional constraints against redistribution to provide "economic justice." In the course of his interview, Obama laid out the electoral strategy of cobbling together the "power coalitions" that have been the hallmark of his 2012 re-election campaign.

Among other things he said during that interview, Obama opined:

> First: "We still suffer from not having a Constitution that guarantees its citizens economic rights." By positive economic rights, Obama means government protection against individual economic failures, such as low incomes, unemployment, poverty, lack of health care, and the like.

Obama characterizes the Constitution as "a charter of negative liberties," which "says what the states can't do to you (and) what the Federal government can't do to you, but doesn't say what the Federal government or State government *must do* on your behalf."

Second, Obama regrets that the Constitution places "essential constraints" on the government's ability to provide positive economic rights and that "we have not broken free" of these Constitutional impediments.

Third, Obama concludes that we cannot use the courts to break free of the limited-government constraints of the Founders. The courts are too tradition and precedent bound "to bring about significant redistributional change."

Fourth, Obama argues that economic rights that the state must supply are ultimately to be established at the ballot box. Those who favor redistribution must gain legislative control through an "actual coalition of powers through which you bring about redistributive change." The electoral task of a redistributive President is therefore to craft coalitions of those who stand to benefit from government largess. The legislature, not the courts, must do this "reparative economic work."

Gregory, writing before the national election of 2012, which gave Obama a second destructive term to achieve the Progressive, "redistributional" agenda, warned:

An Obama electoral victory based on "power coalitions" unconstrained by "negative rights" would fulfill the Founders' dread of an "overbearing majority." As James Madison warned in 1787: "Measures are too often decided, not according to the rules of justice and the rights of the minor party, but by the superior force of an interested and overbearing majority..... If a majority be united by a common interest, the rights of the minority will be insecure."

The Constitution's framers used the separation of powers and the Bill of Rights (most importantly the due process clause of the Fifth Amendment) to render "the overbearing majority ...unable to concert and carry into effect schemes of oppression." It is these "negative rights" that Obama proposes to eliminate. With them disappear restraints on limited government, and anything goes.

And everything has gone. The restraints on Congressional, executive, and federal power row are little more than strings of gossamer, thanks also to a Supreme Court that has lost sight of its purpose. Our rights are no more secure than they would have been in Nazi Germany or Soviet (or Putin's) Russia.

But, there are back-door ways to quash freedom of speech without having to resort to anything as formal as a proposed constitutional amendment. The 2002 McCain-Feingold Campaign Finance Act, which dictates what and when one may speak about candidates for office, ought to have been struck down by the Supreme Court the moment the first suit about its constitutionality was filed. Instead, the Court has simply crippled it with the *Citizens United v. FEC* case.

Dinish D'Souza, a prominent conservative writer and filmmaker, and unabashed critic of Obama and his policies, was charged with violating the Federal Election Commission's rules on donor limits. Paul Bond, in his Hollywood Reporter article of May 20th, "Dinesh D'Souza Pleads Guilty to Making Illegal Campaign Contribution," wrote:

> In exchange for D'Souza's plea, prosecutors are expected to drop the more serious charge of making false statements to the Federal Election Commission, a crime that carries a maximum sentence of five years in prison.

> D'Souza was indicted in January for asking some friends to donate money to the campaign of Wendy Long, a Republican who ran unsuccessfully against Democratic incumbent Sen. Kirsten Gillibrand in New York in 2012, and allegedly promising to reimburse them for their donations.

Bond noted:

From the beginning, attorney Benjamin Brafman characterized his client's alleged transgression as "an act of misguided friendship," and he and others have said federal authorities were engaging in payback for D'Souza's movie *2016: Obama's America*, a hit documentary that portrayed President Barack Obama in a negative light. "

It's a remarkably selective prosecution, considering Obama raised millions of dollars under similar circumstances and donors merely faced civil fines while D'Souza is charged with felony violation of federal law," Sen. Ted Cruz of Texas told *The Hollywood Reporter* in February.

If D'Souza had not pleaded guilty, a trial would have been necessary, and on the "illegal" contribution charge alone, if found guilty, he could have been sentenced to a maximum of two years in prison.

In 1957, Ayn Rand's prophetic novel, *Atlas Shrugged*, was published. It featured, in one chapter, the nature of laws such as the Campaign Finance law. In that chapter, a federal bureaucratic villain, Dr. Floyd Ferris, is trying to blackmail an industrialist into "donating" his new metal to the nation as a "gift." The industrialist is "guilty" of buying more copper than federal law allowed, and also for refusing to honor a federal purchase order for his product. He tells the industrialist:

"Did you think that we want those laws to be observed?" said Dr. Ferris. "We *want* them broken. You'd better get it straight that it's not a bunch of boy scouts you're up against – then you'll know that this is not the age for beautiful gestures. We're after power and we mean it. You fellows were pikers, but we know the real trick, and you'd better get wise to it. There's no way to rule innocent men. The only power any government has is to crack down on criminals. Well, when there aren't enough criminals, one makes them. One declares so many things to be a crime that it becomes impossible for men to live without breaking laws. Who wants a nation of law-abiding citizens? What's there in that for anyone? But just pass the kinds of laws that can neither be observed nor enforced nor objectively interpreted – and you create a nation of lawbreakers – and then you cash in on guilt. Now that's the system, Mr. Rearden, that's the game, and once you understand it, you'll be much easier to deal with."*

And that is the nature of the Campaign Finance law, a law created to shut us up and to punish us if we don't shut up, even if that takes the form of a scream of pain. That is the purpose of Justice Stevens's and Harry Reid's constitutional amendments, to silence the Dinesh D'Souza's of this country. The proposed amendments are not targeted at individuals who "collude" with other individuals to cobble together more than the "allowed" minimum to any organization or candidate. The existing law, together with the proposed amendments, are specifically targeted at prominent individuals such as D'Souza, to make an example of them, so everyone with lesser means will tremble in fear, and fall into line.

The purpose? To preserve and expand the political power of the Democrats, of all the statists in and out of government, by silencing their critics. And that issue is aside from the White House siccing the IRS on conservative groups for not shutting up.

The Progressives, the Left, and the Democrats want to shut us up – warning that if we know what's good for us – such as federal agents not hounding us and taking us to court, or refraining from a plan bash on our skulls – we'll shut up.

Try me.

*P. 436. *Atlas Shrugged*, by Ayn Rand (1957). New York: Dutton/Penguin Books, 1992. 1168 pp.

May 2014

Obama Says: "Shut Up!"

While blaming the federal government's shutdown on the House's dragging its feet on a budget bill that would raise the debt ceiling and defund Obamacare, and not himself or the government itself for "shutting down," President Barack Obama during an address to Congress in the White House State Dining Room on the morning of October 17th displayed his true anti-freedom and anti-freedom of speech colors by blaming bloggers, talk radio hosts and "activists" for the shutdown. It demonstrated his core hostility to freedom in any realm. In short, he would just rather we all shut up and let him get on with destroying the country, and not bother him or anyone else with the least squeak of opposition.

This is the portrait of a wannabe tyrant.

On Thursday Obama took a swipe at freedom of speech. Of the 2,464 words he uttered, these were the most ominous and relevant:

> And now that the government has reopened and this threat to our economy is removed, all of us need to stop focusing on the lobbyists, and the bloggers, and the talking heads on radio and the professional activists who profit from conflict, and focus on what the majority of Americans sent us here to do, and that's grow this economy, create good jobs, strengthen the middle class, educate our kids, lay the foundation for broad-based prosperity and get our fiscal house in order for the long haul. That's why we're here. That should be our focus.

It's a statement so loaded with hypocrisy and venality and undisguised dissimulation, that if awards were given for secular *taqiyya*, Obama would win it hands down. He would easily trounce Richard Nixon, who, in 1973, declared, "I am not a crook."

Andrea Peterson of the Washington Post criticized Obama's remarks, ending her article with:

> But blaming the blogging field for the way the Internet and the entire journalism industry works seems like a bit of a reach -- especially lumping them in with professional

activists and lobbyists who are literally paid to advocate one side or another, as well as partisan talking heads. Is the president trolling us?

He is doing more than "trolling" us, more than challenging us to shut up and be quiet. For the umpteenth time he has bared his teeth at America.

Noah Rothman on Mediate also reported on Obama's "victory" speech:

> Obama went after what he called the "rhetoric" which "gets worse" annually, and for members to focus on where they agree. He cited a "balanced approach" to a budget process as one of these areas of agreement between Democrats and Republicans.
>
> "Had one side not decided to pursue a strategy of brinkmanship, each side could have gotten together and figured out how do we shape a budget that provides certainty to businesses, and people who rely on government?" Obama said.
> He added that "comprehensive immigration reform" and a farm bill should also be the focus of the Congress for the rest of the year.

Can you believe the hubris of this man? Guess which side is guilty of "brinksmanship"? Obama. And the Senate. And that "should"? It sounds more like "You'd better focus on a farm bill and immigration reform, or I'll be very, very angry."

Kurt Nimmo of InfoWars came closest to construing what Obama really meant:

> Following the deal to end the government non-shutdown, Obama took to the podium and teleprompter to excoriate Americans opposed to the staggering bankster and Federal Reserve debt destroying the country.
>
> ...In other words, Obama demands that the American people stop reading sites like Infowars.com and flock over to the corporate Mockingbird media where they can consume a standard fare of government propaganda and lies.

11.

James Taranto at the Wall Street Journal had this to say about Obama's forked tongue:

> Yesterday Obama delivered remarks at the White House, in which he made only an oblique reference to ObamaCare: "You don't like a particular policy or a particular president, then argue for your position. Go out there and win an election. Push to change it. But don't break it. Don't break what our predecessors spent over two centuries building. That's not being faithful to what this country is about."
>
> This is galling for multiple reasons. For one, he was lecturing members of Congress, every one of whom (with the exception of three appointed senators) holds his office by virtue of having won his most recent election. Granted, Obama won his too, but with the help of an abusive IRS. And the country now faces a crisis because in 2009 and 2010, when it came to health care, Obama and his fellow Democrats failed to act in accord with the advice he now dishes out: "Don't break it."

Our predecessors didn't spend over two centuries preparing the way for Obamacare or any other statist legislation. Who's really doing the "breaking"? Obama and the Senate. And, but for a pitiful few in Congress, there isn't a single politician or bureaucrat or Cabinet appointee who either knows what this country is about, or would be faithful to it if he did know.

Unfortunately, the only member of the GOP who came close to arguing against Obamacare in terms of its violation of individual rights was Ted Cruz during a 22-hour standup speech.

I would be thrilled to see Obama, seated with a smug look on his face in the Oval Office, being instructed by Thomas Sowell on the workings of the Constitution, with Harry Reid and all the Democratic Senators standing by, trying not to hear what Sowell was saying:

> There is really noting complicated about the facts [about who was responsible for the shutdown]. The Republican-controlled House of Representatives voted all the money required to keep all government activities going – except for ObamaCare. This is not a matter of opinion. You can check the Congressional Record.

As for the House of Representatives' right to grant or withhold money, that is not a matter of opinion, either. You can check the Constitution of the United States. All spending bills must originate in the House of Representatives, which means that Congressmen there have a right to decide whether or not they want to spend money on a particular government activity....

The Senate chose not to vote to authorize that money to be spent, because it did not include money for ObamaCare.

It's as simple as that. The House did not shut down the government. The Senate did, with the encouragement of the White House.

Obama said last Thursday morning:

Now, there's been a lot of discussion lately of the politics of this shutdown. But let's be clear: There are no winners here. These last few weeks have inflicted completely unnecessary damage on our economy. We don't know yet the full scope of the damage, but every analyst out there believes it slowed our growth.

Speaking of damage to the economy, there is the matter of the fabulously expensive clunker of a website that was supposed to enable citizens to sign up for coverage at the speed of light, beginning with the October 1st "launch." Never mind the fraud behind Obamacare that you can "keep yourplan." That's not true, as a former Secret Service man discovered and had the spine to say publically.

Mr. President,

In one of your famous Obamacare speeches you stated, "If you like your plan, you can keep your plan." Well, as evidenced by the below letter, which my wife and I just received, you lied.

Apparently the former Secret Service man was one of the very, very few able to negotiate his way through the Obamacare website and see the bad news, as well. Daniel Greenfield in a FrontPage article calls it the most incompetent thing Obama has ever done.

The ObamaCare website, which estimates have placed at anywhere from under 100 million to 400 million to just under 300 million to 634 million dollars, not only tops even Solyndra, but couldn't have been designed any worse if Joe Biden had tried making it in his spare time.

The federal health care exchange was built using 10-year-old technology that may require constant fixes and updates for the next six months and the eventual overhaul of the entire system, technology experts told USA TODAY.

The root cause of the problems was a pivotal decision by Centers for Medicare and Medicaid Services officials to act as systems integrator, the central coordinator for the entire program. Usually this role is reserved for the prime information technology contractor.

As a result, full testing of the site was delayed until four to six days before the fateful Oct. 1 launch of the health care exchanges, the individual said.

For those wanting to entrap themselves in the Obamacare website's netherworld, it's a matter of hurry up and wait. The website is worthy of a Road Runner cartoon. Guess who would get to play Wiley Coyote?

On a last economic note, Obama delivered another passel of bare-faced lies.

Let me be specific about three places where I believe we can make progress right now. First, in the coming days and weeks, we should sit down and pursue a balanced approach to a responsible budget, a budget that grows our economy faster and shrinks our long-term deficits further....
And remember, *the deficit is getting smaller, not bigger*. It's going down faster than it has in the last 50 years. The challenges we have right now are not short-term deficits; it's the long-term obligations that we have around things like Medicare and Social Security. We want to make sure those are there for future generations. [*Italics* mine]

14.

Come again? Mr. President, if you are reading this, please go to this link and watch the climbing numbers in the U.S. Debt Clock. Words fail me. But they apparently don't fail you. Words mean nothing to you. They're just devices to fill space and deflect reality.

Au contraire, we bloggers, talking heads, writers, critics, thinkers, and professional activists will *not* shut up. It isn't a president's business to tell people to keep quiet and let the juggernaut of statism roll over them unopposed. And if you try to shut us up...well, Patrick Henry had a few choice words for tyrants who wished to silence his critics. You would do well to remember them.

> "Caesar," said he, "had his Brutus, Charles his Cromwell, and (pausing) George the third (here a cry of treason, treason was heard, supposed to issue from the chair, but with admirable presence of mind he proceeded) may profit by their examples. Sir, if this be treason," he continued, "make the most of it."

October 2013

Stealthy Moves Against Freedom of Speech

Advocates and defenders of the First Amendment and freedom of speech are strung out like the three Roman legions that were ambushed and ultimately annihilated by barbarians in the dense Teutoburg Forest in Germany in 9 A.D. Out of a force of about 36,000 fighting men, the Romans suffered between 16,000 and 20,000 casualties.

The First Amendment, appended to the Constitution with nine other Amendments which became known collectively as the Bill of Rights, reads:

> Congress shall make no law respecting an establishment of religion, or prohibiting the free exercise thereof; or abridging the freedom of speech, or of the press; or the right of the people peaceably to assemble, and to petition the government for a redress of grievances.

And that Amendment is all Americans have at present protecting them from censorship and a dictatorship. We are marching into an ambush by secular advocates of censorship and Islamic ones. Our political leadership is either as ignorant of the perils as were the Roman army's generals, or just as careless in its defense, or oft times even hostile to it.

No European nation has the equivalent of the First Amendment. As Bruce Bawer, an American journalist who has lived in Europe for years, noted in his October 2010 column on the trial of Geert Wilders, the Dutch politician who stood trial for "blaspheming" Islam (and who was subsequently acquitted of all charges):

> One of the most bizarre aspects of being an American in Western Europe — at least if you're an American who has opinions and is used to expressing them freely — is getting accustomed to the fact that there's no First Amendment over here. Some of us grew up thinking of Western Europe as part of the "Free World." But how free is a country if it doesn't recognize freedom of speech as a fundamental right?

Indeed. Just how "free" is the "Free World" when most of its members labor under various gradations of the welfare/regulatory state? The fact is that freedom of speech in Europe is *granted* by the various governments there, but it is a conditional granting by the state, and not a recognized inherent right of the individual. And the conditions are many and malodorous. The chief complainant in Europe has been Islam. Bawer notes:

> In recent years, the superiority of America on this score has been affirmed again and again, as one Western European government after another has prosecuted individuals for saying or writing things that were deemed unacceptable. In a preponderance of cases, these prosecutions have been for statements about Islam. Some of the defendants — Oriana Fallaci, Brigitte Bardot — have been famous.

The superiority of the First Amendment lies in the fact that it expresses a fundamental requirement for existence, while European speech laws deal with incidentals, as though the "right" to express oneself were a spurious privilege, icing on the cake of a government permitting one to live and slave away for the collective. This premise, however, has been introduced into U.S. law in the guise of "hate speech" and "hate crimes."

Now, the problem with "hate speech" is that it is an anti-concept *and* an attempt to read men's minds. I hate Islam. So what? I can explain why I hate Islam, but a rational, and even an irrational explanation is irrelevant to "hate speech" law. So what if I express my "hate" in words or in images? Words and images and even gestures are not metaphysical entities that can be shot, catapulted, or flung at the object of hate. Words, images and gestures do not have the physical power to destroy or harm anything or anyone. Perhaps even a *dhimmi* American judge would concede those points. He should conclude: No *crime* has been committed.

However, if my "hate speech" provokes initiatory force or actions by those claiming defamation or being "hurt" by my speech, it is the "potential" provocation to action for which I could be punished, penalized and even jailed. The "potential" may not even realize itself, but woe to me if Muslims began taking physical action against me and others, resulting in injury, death, or the destruction of property. Look what happened to the "Innocence of Muslims" trailer-maker. His YouTube film was used as an excuse to blame "free speech" for the attack on Benghazi, resulting in the deaths of four Americans. He was arrested, held without bail, and subsequently sentenced to a year in prison. Initially, however, it was our own State Department via Hillary Clinton together with President Barack Obama that assigned the blame. It was later proven that the film had nothing to do with the attack.

Remember what happened after the publication of the Mohammad cartoons? Muslim mayhem. You wouldn't need to calmly examine Islam as a religious or political system. Even should you suggest that Mohammad had lice in his beard and was probably syphilitic, out would come the crazed, semi-literate Muslim hordes demanding your head on a pike. It would make no difference.

My speech could not by any definition be regarded as an initiation of force. But the actions taken by those who wish to punish me, or to suppress it before I have even spoken it – be they Muslims acting on their own, or the government itself on behalf of Muslims – can be. And the question is: Were my words provocative? In the final analysis, *no*. Men are free to agree or disagree with what I say, or even to ignore what I say. Absent any attempt by me to *force* others to hear what I have to say, to read what I have written, or even to acknowledge a physical gesture (such as giving Mohammad an "Italian salute"), then any physical or statutory "retaliation" against me *is* an initiation of force.

Only a government can employ censorship against a nation's citizens, that is, use initiatory force to silence anyone from expressing a viewpoint, disseminating information, voicing opposition to a political system, or even showing a picture. Only a government can "legally" punish an individual for expressing what is on his mind. And it is the *mind* which both a censorial government and groups such as Muslims wish to neutralize or extinguish.

In the U.S. censorship is a mosaic of disparate instances that do not add up to blanket censorship one might otherwise associate with iron-fisted dictatorships like Nazi Germany, Soviet Russia, and Communist/Fascist China. Censorship by private individuals, corporations, newspapers, magazines and the like, however, is *not* censorship: It is the barring of viewpoints, language, images or behavior on nominally private premises, be they pages in a newspaper, over the airwave, physical private property, or an Internet venue (e.g., Facebook), because they are in opposition to the host's viewpoint or violate its rules.

Absent in private "censorship" is the element of force. Individuals do not have a right to force others to act as their soapboxes for viewpoints or behavior others find objectionable or repellent. Nor have they a right to literally force themselves on another's property.

Europe continues to follow the path to a state of affairs concerning speech so restrictive that Europeans may as well not even bother opening their mouths or writing an essay, for the least criticism, especially of Islam, can be interpreted by Muslims and by European Union bureaucrats as "hurtful" or "defamatory" or an expression of "hate."

Soeren Kern, in his October 28th Gatestone article "EU Proposal to Monitor 'Intolerant' Citizens," reported:

> While European leaders are busy expressing public indignation over reports of American espionage operations in the European Union, the European Parliament is quietly considering a proposal that calls for the direct surveillance of any EU citizen suspected of being "intolerant."

> Critics say the measure -- which seeks to force the national governments of all 28 EU member states to establish "special administrative units" to monitor any individual or group expressing views that the self-appointed guardians of European multiculturalism deem to be "intolerant" -- represents an unparalleled threat to free speech in a Europe where citizens are already regularly punished for expressing the "wrong" opinions, especially about Islam.

> The proposed European Framework Statute for the Promotion of Tolerance was recently presented to members of the Civil Liberties, Justice and Home Affairs Committee of the European Parliament, the only directly-elected body of the European Union.

Kern goes on to explain that the focus of the proposed legislation is an unqualified "tolerance" that will not "tolerate" the least criticism of especially Islam, and provides a breakdown of the intent and method of enforcing "tolerance." Importantly, he emphasizes:

> Section 6 states: "It goes without saying that enactment of a Statute for the Promotion of Tolerance does not suffice by

itself. There must be a mechanism in place ensuring that the Statute does not remain on paper and is actually implemented in the world of reality."

An explanatory note to Section 6 (a) states: "Members of vulnerable and disadvantaged groups are entitled to a special protection, additional to the general protection that has to be provided by the Government to every person within the State." Another note adds: "The special protection afforded to members of vulnerable and disadvantaged groups may imply a preferential treatment. Strictly speaking, this preferential treatment goes *beyond mere respect and acceptance lying at the root of tolerance.*" [*Italics* mine]

The "reality" in Europe is that Islam is setting the terms of every European's political existence. One after another, national and local governments capitulate to demands by Muslims that they be accommodated in terms of mosque construction, blaring calls to prayers, closing off public streets for mass prayers, the serving of Islamic *halal* food in schools and other "public" venues, and numerous other "concessions" to Islamic mores (such as they are).

Who actually are the new "members of vulnerable and disadvantaged groups"? Non-Muslims. What do the architects of Islam's "preferential treatment" expect of non-Muslims "beyond mere respect and acceptance"? The total surrender of their minds and obsequious submission not only to Islam, but to the EU's totalitarian dictats. The Soviets, by forbidding and punishing all instances of independent thought, hoped to nurture the creation of a "Soviet Man," that is, an automaton that would unthinkingly do the Party's bidding. The EU hopes its speech suppression laws will produce the "Tolerant Person," an automaton that will "tolerate" its own destruction by being assimilated into Islamic society.

Jacob Mchangama, in an analysis of the origin and implementation of "hate speech" law in his December 2011 Hoover Institution paper, "The Sordid Origin of Hate-Speech Laws," writes that, indeed, hate speech laws are a legacy of Soviet totalitarianism:

All western European countries have hate-speech laws. In 2008, the EU adopted a framework decision on "Combating Racism and Xenophobia" that obliged all member states to criminalize certain forms of hate speech. On the other side of the Atlantic, the Supreme Court of the United States has gradually increased and consolidated the protection of hate speech under the First Amendment. The European concept of freedom of expression thus prohibits certain content and viewpoints, whereas, with certain exceptions, the American concept is generally concerned solely with direct incitement likely to result in overt acts of lawlessness.

Yet the origin of hate-speech laws has been largely forgotten. *The divergence between the United States and European countries is of comparatively recent origin.* In fact, the United States and the vast majority of European (and Western) states were originally opposed to the internationalization of hate-speech laws. European states and the U.S. shared the view that human rights should protect rather than limit freedom of expression. [*Italics* mine]

Rather, the introduction of hate-speech prohibitions into international law was championed in its heyday by the Soviet Union and allies. Their motive was readily apparent. The communist countries sought to exploit such laws to limit free speech.

That "divergence" between Europe and the U.S. is shrinking to a state of *convergence.*

Bruce Bawer also weighed in on the proposed legislation in his October 30th FrontPage article, "EU Unveils Crackdown on Free Speech."

The first thing I ever wrote about Islam was an essay for *Partisan Review* entitled "Tolerating Intolerance," which was published a few months after 9/11. My argument, in brief, was that Islam is not just a religion but an ideology that teaches an extreme and violent intolerance – and that Europeans had a right to protect the freedom of their societies by implementing well-informed immigration and integration policies. Now the European Council on Tolerance and Reconciliation (ECTR), founded in 2008 and consisting largely of former European presidents or prime ministers, has issued a report whose thrust is – and I quote – that there's "no need to be tolerant to the intolerant."

21.

But the argument of the report – which was presented to the European Parliament in late September and takes the form of a "Model Statute for Tolerance" that the ECTR hopes to see enacted by all EU member states, is light-years away from the one I made all those years ago in *Partisan Review*. The ECTR's concern is not with addressing the importation into Europe of Islamic intolerance but, rather, with addressing the purported intolerance of Europeans toward (among other things) imported Islam.

President Barack Obama pronounced at the U.N.. in September 2012, "The future must not belong to tose who slander the prophet of Islam" But the future seems to belong to Muslims and Western judges who would persecute anyone who gave Islam and Mohammad a scholarly or visceral middle finger. To Islam, everything said about Mohammad by infidels is "slanderous."

Cooperating with the European Parliament is the Organization of Islamic Cooperation (OIC), with its recent Geneva Conference on speech and its United Nations Resolution 16/18, which seeks to ban and punish all "defamatory" speech, most and especially about or against Islam.

Deborah Weiss reported on October 22nd in her FrontPage article, "Geneva Conference Moves Toward Criminalizing 'Islamophobia'."
In its quest to criminalize speech that's critical of all Islam-related topics, the Organization of Islamic Cooperation (OIC)* endorsed the formation of a new Advisory Media Committee to address "Islamophobia."

> This past September, the OIC held "The First International Conference on Islamophobia: Law & Media." The conference endorsed numerous recommendations which arose from prior workshops on Islamophobia from media, legal and political perspectives. A main conclusion was the consensus to institutionalize the conference and create an Advisory Media Committee to meet under the newly established OIC Media Forum based in Istanbul Turkey.

Note that the conference was not held to discuss the criminalization of "Judeophobia" or "Christophobia" or even "Atheistiophobia."

Supposedly, the purpose of the conference was to support an OIC campaign to "correct the image of Islam and Muslims in Europe and North America." By this, it means to whitewash the intolerant, violent and discriminatory aspects of Islam and Islamists. The OIC has launched a campaign to provide disinformation to the public, delinking all Islam from these undesirable traits and attacks all who insist on these truths, as bigots, racists and Islamophobes....Its present goal is the international criminalization of all speech that "defames" Islam, which the OIC defines as anything that sheds a negative light on Islam or Muslims, even when it's true (wrote Clare Lopez in American Thinker in 2011 in 2011).

Its target is the West and one of its tactics is to accuse those who criticize Islam or its various interpretations as "Islamophobic." It is attempting to pass the equivalent of Islamic blasphemy codes in the West, using accusations of bigotry to silence anyone who speaks the truth about Islamic terrorism or Islamic persecution of religious minorities.

The OIC wants enforceable laws passed in Western nations that complement its wish to criminalize speech regarding Islam. In practice, this would mean that only Islamic clerics and spokesmen would be allowed to say anything about Islam. And Muslims, treated as "victimized" minorities in those nations, would be free to persecute, murder, rape, and terrorize Jews, Christians, atheists and other non-Muslims with impunity and indemnity everywhere and any time they wished. As they do now.

Can such Orwellian laws be passed in this country? The existence of "hate speech" and "hate crime" judicial decisions in American courts has prepared the ground for them here. It was Secretary of State Hillary Clinton who invited OIC members to a conference in Washington to discuss how American law can conform to U.N. Resolution 16/18 and the OIC agenda. What difference can it make to her if Americans are gagged and threatened with prosecution for speaking out against Islam or drawing to the public's attention the gruesome facts of Islam in practice and in action?

Just remember, and to paraphrase that Orwellian warning: "Hate speech" *is* "hate crime." Just ask Audrey Hudson, the journalist whose home was raided by Federal and Maryland state law enforcement in search of evidence of her own "hate crime."

And so began Hudson's nightmare – held captive by armed agents of the U.S. Coast Guard, Maryland State Police and the Department of Homeland Security as they staged a pre-dawn raid in search of unregistered firearms and a "potato gun."

"I think they found a great way to get into my house and get a hold of my confidential notes and go through every other file in my office." - Audrey Hudson, journalist

But instead of taking the potato gun, agents seized unrelated government documents and notes from the former Washington Times journalist.

Agents took Hudson's records during a search for guns and related items owned by her husband, a civilian Coast Guard employee. They also confiscated her legally registered firearms, according to court documents obtained by the Associated Press.

The lesson here is that a search warrant no longer is a protection against the depredations of any government agency that has the power to expropriate one's property, or to intimidate anyone who has been critical of government policies, gaffes, failures and tyrannical behavior. Search warrants are now just a pretext to violate one's person and one's rights. The barbarians and totalitarians inside and outside our borders are ready to ambush the First Amendment and render us helpless against their onslaught.

October 2013

The Peril of "Hate Crimes"

A totalitarian anti-concept of "justice" has been gnawing away at objective law without correction or opposition, and making rapid progress in a judicial system that has steadily abandoned reason and the protection of individual rights: *hate crime*.

Hate crimes initially were violations of individual rights motivated by the perpetrators' hatred of a victim's race, gender, religion, or political affiliation. Hatred is an emotion that can be traced to two fundamental evaluations: fear, and malice. One can justifiably hate what one fears, if what one fears jeopardizes a rational value or one's life. Or, one can hate what one fears because it threatens an irrational value, such as blind faith or one's purported racial or cultural superiority. Malice is simply a raw, unreasoning hatred of a good for being the good.

But the motivating, emotional element of a demonstrable or provable violation of an individual's right (murder, rape, physical assault) has been factored into the severity of a defendant's crime and in consequent punishment after his conviction and trial.

In short, the *why* of a crime is increasingly treated as though it were a weapon, such as a gun, a knife, or a club. In standard criminal cases, however, it has never been the instrument of crime that was on trial, but the defendant and his *actions*.

Proponents of hate crime have attempted to find a compromise between objectivity in criminal law and the notion that a felon should also be punished for what caused him to commit the crime. But no such compromise is feasible if objective law is to be preserved and justice served. The irrational element – that is, making thought, however irrational or ugly it may be, a crime – has suborned the rational. No compromise between good and evil is lasting or practical. Evil will always come out the victor.

It did not take long for the corrupting notion of hate crimes to degenerate into *thought crime*. This is what happens when reason is declared irrelevant or is abandoned or diluted by the irrational.

It used to be that a criminal was sentenced for his crime, and if the crime was committed from some form of prejudice, the court's and jury's afterthought was usually: And, by the way, your motives are contemptible and despicable.

Appended now to a guilty verdict for the murder of an individual because of his race, gender "orientation," religion, or political affiliation, is another verdict: You have no right to think that way, so we are adding five years to your sentence and adding X amount to your monetary penalty.

A salutary instance of the corruption of justice is the Rutgers University "hate crime" case. The New York Times, in September 2010, reported:

> It started with a Twitter message on Sept. 19: "Roommate asked for the room till midnight. I went into molly's room and turned on my webcam. I saw him making out with a dude. Yay."

> That night, the authorities say, the Rutgers University student who sent the message used a camera in his dormitory room to stream the roommate's intimate encounter live on the Internet.

> And three days later, the roommate who had been surreptitiously broadcast — Tyler Clementi, an 18-year-old freshman and an accomplished violinist — jumped from the George Washington Bridge into the Hudson River in an apparent suicide....

> The Middlesex County prosecutor's office said Mr. Clementi's roommate, Dharun Ravi, 18, of Plainsboro, N.J., and another classmate, Molly Wei, 18, of Princeton Junction, N.J., had each been charged with two counts of invasion of privacy for using "the camera to view and transmit a live image" of Mr. Clementi. The most serious charges carry a maximum sentence of five years.

In many states, invasion of privacy is a misdemeanor, not a capital crime. Dharun Ravi was originally charged with invasion of privacy. But the alleged "hate crime" against a gay metastasized into a de facto trial for committing a capital crime, because Clementi committed suicide. Ravi was not charged with Clementi's murder, but it was implied that he was responsible for his suicide.

Fast forward to March, 2012. The presiding judge in the case contributed to the confusion;

The Times reported:

> The jury in the trial of a former Rutgers University student accused of invading his roommate's privacy by using a webcam to watch him in an intimate encounter began deliberations on Wednesday and asked the judge to define two crucial terms.
>
> Jurors asked Judge Glenn Berman of Superior Court in Middlesex County to restate the definition of "intimidate," as well as of the word "purpose," as it related to the bias intimidation count.
>
> The judge ruled that the defendant, Dharun Ravi, could be found guilty of *bias intimidation* only if he was also found guilty of the first charge, *invasion of privacy*. And he told the jury that the roommate, Tyler Clementi, would have been the victim of bias intimidation if he had been made to feel fear. [*Italics* mine.]
>
> "A person is guilty of the crime of bias intimidation," Judge Berman said, "if he commits an offense with the purpose to intimidate an individual because of sexual orientation."
>
> Mr. Ravi is charged with 15 counts, including bias intimidation, invasion of privacy and tampering with evidence. Prosecutors say he encouraged friends to view a feed from his webcam that showed Mr. Clementi with another man. Mr. Clementi committed suicide shortly afterward, in September 2010.

There are several things wrong with this. First, Clementi learned of the webcam prank indirectly by reading Ravi's Twitter posts about him (thirty-eight times). Ravi was not attempting to "intimidate Clementi, or "bully" him. Hi-tech back-fence gossip and slander-mongering about another person are not "intimidation." Ravi invited his friends to watch the webcam, not Clementi. Secondly, no one knows why Clementi committed suicide. He left a brief, cryptic suicide note which shed no light on *his* motive. ABC News reported:

> Former Rutgers student Dharun Ravi was told by police that his text message apology for spying on roommate Tyler Clementi was written within minutes of Clementi's suicide note.
>
> In a taped interview with investigators the day after Clementi's suicide Ravi is seen struggling to understand as he is told that his apology to Clementi was received just minutes before Clementi posted a Facebook message saying, "Jumping off the gw bridge sorry."
>
> "Did he get that text before?" Ravi asked investigators.
>
> "That's the way it looks," an officer responded.
>
> "So he got mine, and then sent his?" Ravi asked, to which the investigators responded yes.
>
> The police, however, appear to have made a mistake. Time stamps on the two messages show that Clementi posted his suicide note at 8:42 p.m. on Sept. 22, 2010. Ravi's apology to Clementi was sent at 8:46 p.m. It's not clear if Clementi ever saw the apology.

But, because no one had or could have had access to the contents of Ravi and Clementi's minds, the jurors, per Judge Berman's instructions and "clarification," were left to resort to second-guessing. To wit:

> What the jury had to decide…was what Mr. Ravi and Mr. Clementi were thinking.
>
> Had Mr. Ravi set up the webcam because he had a pretty good idea that he would see Mr. Clementi in an intimate moment? Had he targeted Mr. Clementi and the man he was with because they were gay? And had Mr. Clementi been in fear?

Without Mr. Clementi to speak for himself, that last question was perhaps the most difficult to determine, and jurors struggled with it.

"That was the hardest because you really can't get into someone's head," said one, Bruno Ferreira, as he left the court. The jury deliberated longest — for well more than an hour, he said — on the bias intimidation charge. [*Italics* mine]

Mr. Ferreira said he ultimately voted guilty on the bias intimidation charge because Mr. Ravi had sent multiple Twitter messages about Mr. Clementi.

So, Ferreira overrode his initial doubts about getting into someone's head by substituting a number and translating it into a motive, or "bias intimidation." No one knows why Ravi engaged in his admittedly malicious prank. No one knows if Clementi committed suicide over the webcam incidents or because he was embarrassed or shamed or just in a suicidal mood. Any one of those reasons is more credible than is the "intimidation" charge.

But Bruce J. Kaplan, the prosecutor in Middlesex County, applauded the jury for sending a strong message against bias. "They felt the pain of Tyler," he said.

No, they were not. The jurors were projecting what they imagined Clementi's emotional state might have been because they were persuaded by the prosecution that Ravi's webcam actions contributed to Clementi's decision to commit suicide. There were no photos of Clementi's anguished state for them to judge, and so no way to even deduce why he was feeling "pain."

I am not taking Ravi's side here. I am taking a stand against the whole notion of hate crimes. If you want to see how a jury properly treats a bigot, watch *Twelve Angry Men* (start here at 1.18.56).

In criminal law, and even in Perry Mason TV law, determining a motive is merely a means to determine the reason for a criminal action, whether it is murder or larceny or petty theft. It was never criminalized itself. Motives exist in men's minds and can not be taken out and paraded as evidence.

29.

Even if they could be, in the past they would not have counted. It was the criminal *action* that was actionable in law, not why a crime was committed. That is changing, for the worse. Motives can not hurt anyone; only an action spurred by a motive, just as guns don't (volitionally) kill people; it is people using guns that kill people. The same logic applies to butter knives, rubber bands, spit balls, or rocks. Guns, butter knives, rubber bands, spit balls and rocks are not imbued with magical powers that force people to commit crimes with them. But gun control advocates wish to pretend that guns have magical powers to turn people into criminals.

Emotions and motives alone are not physical objects that can harm anyone.

Emotions are evaluations, and evaluations are products of thought. To condemn and punish an emotion is to criminalize thought. It's as simple as that. Crime enters the picture only when one acts on the emotion. The action is demonstrable.

The guiltiest party in this affair is <u>Judge Glenn Berman</u>, who aided and abetted in the sanctioning of "hate crimes" and "bias intimidation," both of which are anti-reason and anti-rights. A judge ought to know the difference between an actual, proven crime in which action is the evidence of a crime, and the contents of an individual's mind. The contents of the mind are no government's or court's business.

A motive or an emotion may help authorities to find clues to a crime or even identify a felon. But it is not a chargeable offense; it is the action stemming from it.

The *why* of a crime is not the crime. It is the action that is the crime. One can deduce, or collect evidence that a person wanted to embezzle his employer's bank accounts, that was his purpose; that is the "why." The crime is the embezzlement, the action, not the motive. The *why* of a crime may deserve condemnation, but it is not the proper object of criminal justice.

But, what has spurred te spread of "hate crime" and "hate speech"? In a word: *tribalism*.

Hate crimes are a direct result of a nation's population scrambling to join tribes based on race, gender, religion, and political affiliation, and these in turn splinter into sub-tribes. Such tribalism is possible in a nation that has abandoned reason and objective law, and a contest ensues in which the various tribes jockey in politics and fiat power to become the dominant and ruling group at the expense of all others.

Novelist/philosopher Ayn Rand about tribalism:

> Tribalism (which is the best name to give to all the group manifestations of the anti-conceptual mentality) is a dominant element in Europe, as a reciprocally reinforcing cause and result of Europe's long history of caste systems, of national and local (provincial) chauvinism, of rule by brute force and endless, bloody wars. As an example, observe the Balkan nations, which are perennially bent upon exterminating one another over minuscule differences of tradition or language. Tribalism had no place in the United States—until recent decades. It could not take root here, its imported seedlings were withering away and turning to slag in the melting pot whose fire was fed by two inexhaustible sources of energy: individual rights and objective law; these two were the only protection man needed.

As the scope of government power grows, so do the number of "tribes" grow to protect themselves from it or to demand a share of it or simply to clamor for a granting of special privileges and status. Today there innumerable tribes locked in constant warfare in response to government power: smokers vs. non- and anti-smokers, gays vs. heterosexuals, blacks vs. whites and/or Asians, Hispanics vs. whites and/or blacks, cyclists vs. motorists, developers vs. conservationists, Christians vs. atheists, and, most prominent of all, Muslims vs. all non-Muslims, and especially Jews.

The last category is particularly vicious because Islam is a totalitarian ideology naturally comfortable, in Sharia law, with the notions of "hate speech" and "hate crime," because the growing ubiquity of such notions in U.S. secular law helps to insulate Islam from Western norms while its activists follow an agenda of conquest or stealth *jihad*. And, the New Black Panthers offered a $10,000 bounty for the "capture" of George Zimmerman, which is in addition to race hustlers like Al Sharpton and Jesse Jackson calling Zimmerman's shooting of a black teenager "racist" and fomenting racial strife.

(It is noteworthy that neither the government nor courts nor the MSM is willing to charge black activists with "hate speech" or "hate crimes." Vociferous black activists are now a "protected" tribe able to slander, libel, and promote malice with impunity.)

As "hate speech" focuses on the written or spoken word (or on "forbidden" images of Mohammad), "hate crime" focuses on thought, whether or not it is spoken or written. You can be sure that the Council on American-Islamic Relations and other Islamic front groups will be looking for ways to exploit the Rutgers precedent. And is certain that ambitious censors in government, such as Cass Sunstein, the "Speech Czar," will also be on the alert for opportunities to silence critics of the current administration based on the Rutgers verdict.

The Rutgers verdict against Ravi does not auger well for the state of criminal justice. Together with the vile notion of "hate speech," "hate crime" is another assault on man's mind.

*"The Missing Link" (1973), in *Philosophy: Who Needs It*," by Ayn Rand. New York: Dutton/Signet, 1982. p. 42.

May 2012

The Perils of "Hate" Speech and Crime Revisited

Defense attorney and seasoned trial lawyer <u>Perry Mason</u> never lost a case to a prosecutor who charged his clients with "hate speech" or with a "hate crime." Or at least no defendant of Mason's was every indicted, charged with, tried for, or found guilty of it. That is because the concepts of "hate speech" and "hate crimes" would never have been admitted by the presiding judge. Indeed, prosecutors would have found the concepts alien, inadmissible, and incompatible with objective law, as well. At least, that would have been the finding in lawyer Erle Stanley Gardner's time, and therefore in Perry Mason's time.

Both Mason and his usual opponent at the bar, District Attorney Hamilton Burger, while they might have dwelt on a defendant's emotions – vengeance, jealousy, avarice, anger, bitterness – in their argumentation, they knew that it was not a defendant's emotions that were on trial, but his actions. It is an action that is a demonstrable thing, not a person's reason for taking an action, except through a person's confession. And even then, it is not a person's reason or motive for committing (or not committing) a crime that is the focus of Mason and Burger, but the action itself.

As I wrote in one of my columns, <u>The Peril of "Hate Crimes,</u>"

> "A totalitarian anti-concept of 'justice' has been gnawing away at objective law without correction or opposition, and making rapid progress in a judicial system that has steadily abandoned reason and the protection of individual rights: *hate crime*."

"Hate" crimes initially were violations of individual rights motivated by the perpetrators' hatred of a victim's race, gender, religion, or political affiliation. The nature of the motive was acknowledged, but was not the subject of a trial. Hatred is an emotion that can be traced to two fundamental evaluations: fear, and malice. One can justifiably hate what one fears, if what one fears jeopardizes a rational value or one's life. Or, one can hate what one fears because it threatens an irrational value, such as blind faith or one's purported racial or cultural superiority. Malice is simply a raw, unreasoning hatred of a good for being the good.

But the motivating, emotional elements of a demonstrable or provable violation of an individual's right (murder, rape, physical assault) are now frequently factored into the severity of a defendant's crime and in consequent punishment after his conviction and trial.

In short, the *why* of a crime is increasingly treated as though it were a weapon, such as a gun, a knife, or a club, or as a kind of co-conspirator or accomplice to a crime. In standard criminal cases, however, it has never been the instrument of crime that was on trial, but the defendant and his *actions*. Until recently, no person or criminal, to my knowledge, has been indicted, convicted, and tried because of his irrationality, only for his irrational actions and his employment of force or fraud to pursue his ends.

I was moved to revisit the subjects of "hate" speech and "hate" crime by an article on Spiked, by Joanna Williams, "Teaching Students to Fear Free Speech," in which she observes, when commenting on the restrictive "free speech" codes at Britain's Exeter University and other British universities:

> Exeter University, like many others, uses the Equality Act to reinterpret freedom of speech as meaning the freedom not to be offended. As Greg Lukianoff puts it in *Unlearning Liberty: Campus Censorship and the End of American Debate*: 'By following a "sensitivity for everyone" as opposed to a "free speech for everyone" model, you create the risk that nobody will be allowed to say anything interesting at all.'

Not even that knight of "social and economic justice," Franklin D. Roosevelt, included, among his vaunted political soufflé of the Four Freedoms (freedom of speech, freedom of worship, freedom from want, freedom from fear), the notion in that check-off list that anyone was entitled to freedom from offense, disparagement, insult, insensitive remarks, distress, verbal abuse, disrespect, and blasphemy, aside from freedom from legitimate scholarly criticism of his economic programs or from satirical attention to the evident hypocrisy of members of his administration. FDR was such an amoral pragmatist I'm sure that were a Muslim or modern day diversity-obsessed leftie close at hand, he could have persuaded FDR to include one or all of Islam's favorite victimhood cards, together with those of the lesbian/gay/transgender/cross-dressing brigade, as well. And that would have been quite a feat of political agenda "diversity."

There are students who have been brow-beaten into not risking voicing criticism of or venturing an opinion on just about anything lest they be upbraided or hauled into a kangaroo court, and there are British sandwich shop owners who make jokes on Facebook about deceased tyros and tin pot dictators. Walter Olson reported on the <u>Overlawyered</u> site on December 14th:

> Authorities in Rugeley, Staffordshire, England, detained sandwich shop owner Neil Phillips for eight hours, searched his computer, fingerprinted him and swabbed him for DNA after a local elected official complained that Phillips had engaged in online jokes and comments on Facebook, including jokes about Nelson Mandela. [<u>Birmingham Mail</u>, <u>The Star</u>] Afterward, Phillips complained that the constabulary had "over-reacted massively": "There was no hatred. What happened to freedom of speech?"

Charles Cooke <u>explains at NRO</u>:

> Well, the Public Order Act of 1986 happened to freedom of speech – in particular, Section 5, which makes it a crime in England for anyone "with intent to cause a person harassment, alarm or distress" to
>
> *(a) [use] threatening, abusive or insulting words or behaviour, or disorderly behaviour, or (b) [display] any writing, sign or other visible representation which is threatening, abusive or insulting, thereby causing that or another person harassment, alarm or distress.*
>
> In other words, Section 5 allows anybody to have anybody else investigated for speaking. And they have. The arrests have run the gamut: from Muslims criticizing atheists to atheists criticizing Muslims....

And that's what happens in Britain to someone who says something interesting. Except to Muslims, Welfare Statists, and Leftists of every stripe, who regularly use threatening, abusive, and insulting words and behavior, and indulge in disorderly behavior, and religiously display writing, signs and other visible representations that are threatening, abusive and insulting, causing upholders of freedom and Western civilization harassment, alarm and distress. Upholders of freedom and Western civilization need not bother filing a complaint, as a politician did against the hapless Neil Phillips.

But, what harm can words cause? First, let's settle on a definition of *word*. In her groundbreaking work, *Introduction to Objectivist Epistemology**, novelist/philosopher Ayn Rand wrote:

> A definition is a statement that identifies the nature of the units subsumed under a concept.
>
> It is often said that definitions state the meaning of words. This is true, but it is not exact. A word is merely a visual-auditory symbol used to represent a concept; a word has no meaning other than that of the concept it symbolizes, and the meaning of a concept consists of its units. It is not words, but concepts that man defines—by specifying their referents.
>
> The purpose of a definition is to distinguish a concept from all other concepts and thus to keep its units differentiated from all other existents.
>
> Since the definition of a concept is formulated in terms of other concepts, it enables man, not only to identify and *retain* a concept, but also to establish the relationships, the hierarchy, the *integration* of all his concepts and thus the integration of his knowledge. Definitions preserve, not the chronological order in which a given man may have learned concepts, but the *logical* order of their hierarchical interdependence.
>
> With certain significant exceptions, every concept can be defined and communicated in terms of other concepts. The exceptions are concepts referring to sensations, and metaphysical axioms. [p. 40]

Building on that, "hate" speech is a concept that, socially and politically, enables a person or the state to treat one's *motive* as a punishable crime, or a *thought* (or emotion) as socially and legally impermissible, and also punishable. "Hate" speech treats words and emotions as literal physical entities capable of inflicting physical, but chiefly emotional or mental harm on another. "Hate" speech regards words as palpable forces that can effect change or trigger unwanted emotions, as though they were hammers tapping on a person's kneecap and causing the lower leg to jerk upward.

Because words – which constitute speech – are merely audio-visual symbols of a thing for which there is a concept, they have no existential, physical attributes or character. Because they have no existential qualities, they cannot by themselves harm or affect anyone or anything. Nor can images. This is why it is humorous to watch someone coax or curse a recalcitrant engine that won't start.

"Hate" crimes, on the other hand, are directly linked to "hate" speech because it is the motives or the contents of one's mind in the context of a provable crime that are targeted for disapprobation. The concept of a "hate" crime refers to actions of a thought carried out in action, and moves it from moral condemnation to a chargeable crime. George Orwell anticipated the phenomenon when he devised the notion of *thoughtcrime* for his dystopian novel, *Nineteen Eighty-Four*.

In a Perry Mason court, if a defendant is on trial for murder, it may be revealed that he wanted the victim's money or wife or prestige, or because the victim was going to disclose his embezzlement or other kind of malfeasance (and may or may not have intended to blackmail the defendant), and so took an immoral action. But his *wanting* something is not what he is on trial for. A Perry Mason court focused on actions taken in pursuit of some gain, or committed in vengeance, and so on.

"Hate" speech, coupled with "hate" crime, are the Gog and Magog of statism and corrupters of genuine justice. They are the twin harbingers of totalitarianism. The U.S. is moving haltingly in that direction, as witness the invocation of "hate" speech" in many judicial decisions as reason and objective law are abandoned in favor of positive law. Britain and Europe are galloping in that direction.

Mark Hendrickson noted in his Forbes Magazine article of May 30th, *The Pandora's Box of Progressivism: Positive Law*:

> The classical liberal view of individual rights being primary and justice consisting of government and law being for the purpose of impartially upholding those rights no longer prevails. It has been supplanted by the notion—advanced by

progressives, socialists, and adherents of various other illiberal ideologies—that government should act in a positive way to make life better for people....Once Americans started to accept the notion that government should lend a helping hand, the potential expansion of government's scope and power became unlimited.

The most recent and notorious example of "positive law" is ObamaCare, which is intended to lend Americans a "helping hand" with their health care insurance. Other examples are anti-smoking laws, anti-trans-fats laws, anti-discrimination laws, and EPA regulations. Positive law or "progressive" law is practiced by a government which sees itself as an "activist" for social legislation and which enacts laws to advance the "common good." It is an enemy of natural law.

"Hate" speech and "hate" crime are intrusive legal examples of positive law, imposed to guarantee an individual's or a group's "freedom from" something that might hurt feelings or a tenuous self-respect.

There would be no room for a Perry Mason in a judicial system that universally adopted "hate" law. He would retire from his practice, knowing that the "positive" law of "hate" speech and "hate" crime could only have a *negative* impact on justice. He might even suspect that justice was not an end or a goal of the proponents of "hate" law, but something rather more insidious: censorship, and the shackling of the human mind.

*From Chapter 5, "Definitions." Ayn Rand, *Introduction to Objectivist Epistemology*. Harry Binswanger and Leonard Peikoff, eds. (1966-1967).New York: Meridian/Penguin, 1990.

December 2013

Politics

Pearls of James Madison, Founder

"Do not give what is holy to the dogs; nor cast your pearls before swine, lest they trample them under their feet, and turn and tear you in pieces." Matthew 7:6

I have little occasion to quote the Bible, and have serious doubts about who first penned or uttered this maxim, coming as it does from a translation of the Bible from the old Latin text to the Vulgate, a task which reputedly engaged several apocryphal hands over the course of centuries. But, Matthew seemed an appropriate place to start, because it is arguably a pearl of wisdom.

We move on to the first set of pearls.

The two premier publishers in the U.S. for books of unmatched quality in terms of printing, design, affordability, and readability, are the Liberty Fund of Indianapolis, and the Library of America in New York.

The Liberty Fund specializes in publishing books about the history, progress, investigation, and value of liberty, and boasts an impressive catalogue of works from the high Renaissance throughout the Enlightenment, and the 18th, 19th and 20th centuries. It is completely private, founded by a businessman, Pierre F. Goodrich, in 1960, and is sustained by sales and donations from individuals of means. Its most recent quarterly catalogue boasts eight pages of some 720 titles, authors and editors, from Lord Acton to Simone Zurbuchen. Its mission statement page states:

> Liberty Fund, Inc. is a private, educational foundation established to encourage the study of the ideal of a society of free and responsible individuals. The Foundation develops, supervises, and finances its own educational activities to foster thought and encourage discourse on enduring issues pertaining to liberty.

The Library of America, on the other hand, was founded in 1979 with "seed money" from the National Endowment for the Humanities, itself established by Congress in 1965. Its purpose is to preserve the literature of America. It published its first volumes in 1982. While I oppose government subsidies for any literary or artistic project, the Library of America, which is now an independent non-profit organization, seems to have been one of the government's more successful investments. It, too, sustains itself by sales and private donations, and, as far as I could determine, receives no federal subsidies of any kind. Its mission statement reads:

> The Library of America, a nonprofit publisher, is dedicated to publishing, and keeping in print, authoritative editions of America's best and most significant writing.

I would say it has republished and kept in print many of America's best and worst writers. Its titles are in the hundreds. Many are indeed worth reading. Some titles can legitimately be deemed "best." Others are the favorites of the literary establishment, not necessarily "best" or even "good." It also publishes a quarterly catalogue with new titles.

But what sets Liberty Fund and Library of America books apart from mainstream publishing is the meticulous attention both publishers pay to book design, organization, and text. I have read several titles from both publishers and I think I found perhaps two typos or errata in over 5,000 pages. And both publishers print their books to last, hard backs and soft covers. They can be perused repeatedly for years with little evidence of wear. Barring book-burnings or bannings by neo-Nazis, Progressives, or Muslims, these books will be around for a long, long time.

(What is not a typo, but an isolated problem with word or line spacing, occurs in Library of America's *James Madison: Writings*,* on page 89, the first page of "The Virginia Plan: Resolutions Proposed by Mr. Randolph in Convention, May 29, 1787." The problem does not recur elsewhere in the text.)

Having said that, we move on to the second set of pearls to be found in that volume. I was reviewing notes I took while first reading *James Madison: Writings*. Here I offer some random pearls of political wisdom from America's <u>fourth president</u>, dubbed the "Father of the Constitution" and "Father of the Bill of Rights." These pearls are particularly relevant today. Wise Americans should learn their value.

Aside from having been a prolific contributor to the <u>Federalist Papers</u>, Madison was a frequent speaker at the <u>Constitutional Convention</u>, held in Philadelphia between May and September, 1787. Madison spoke from written notes, or extemporaneously, and his (and others') remarks were recorded in shorthand by a clerk reporter. As with Thomas Jefferson and some other notable Founders, Madison was not the compelling orator as Patrick Henry was. Often his remarks were inaudible, and the assembly of delegates and reporters could not hear what he said.

Speaking on the role of what would eventually become the U.S. Supreme Court and its relationship with the two other branches of the federal government, the executive and the legislative, Madison said:

> In England...the Executive had an absolute negative on the laws; and the supreme tribunal of Justice (the House of Lords) formed one of the other branches of the Legislature. In short, whether the object of the revisionary power to restrain the Legislature from encroaching on the other coordinate Departments, or on the rights of the people at large; or from passing laws unwise in their principle, or incorrect in their form, the utility of annexing the wisdom and weight of the Judiciary to the Executive seemed incontestable. (p. 95)

The next day, June 7th, Madison spoke of the function and composition of what would become the U.S. Senate, which was established primarily to act as a brake on populist legislation arising in the House of

Representatives, and secondarily as a presence of the states' legislatures, who elected each Senator:

> The use of the Senate is to consist in its proceeding with more coolness, with more system, and with more wisdom, than the popular branch. Enlarge their number and you communicate the vices which they are meant to correct.

The function and character of the U.S. Senate were obliterated with passage of the 17th Amendment and its ratification by the states in 1913. The U.S. Senate was a party to its own neutering. For all practical purposes – and given its conduct in recent decades – the U.S. Senate became a legislative auxiliary of the House, in effect enlarging the size of the House, and defeating the Senate's fundamental purposes. 1913 was a watershed year in U.S. politics, with passage of the 16th Amendment (the Income Tax Amendment), the establishing of the Federal Reserve System, and ratification of the 17th Amendment.

Madison and his colleagues at the Constitutional Convention could hardly have imagined that 129 years after the Constitution was ratified, it would be largely nullified by statist policies empowered by a president, Woodrow Wilson, and his administration, and by Congress itself.

There is a somewhat anemic movement reported in some blog sites to press Congress to impeach Barack Obama. I think these will come to naught. However, Madison, on July 20, 1787, was recorded by the clerk as saying:

> Mr. Madison thought it indispensable that some provision should be made for defending the Community against the incapacity, negligence or perfidy of the chief Magistrate [the President]. The limitation of the period of his service, was not a sufficient security. He might lose his capacity after his appointment. He might pervert his administration into a scheme of peculation or oppression. He might even betray his trust to foreign powers….(p. 128, square brackets mine)

These words, excepting the provision for the incapacitation of the President, could describe the candidacy for impeachment of virtually every president from FDR onward. They especially apply to Barack Obama.

It could not be presumed that all or even a majority of an Assembly would either lose their capacity for discharging, or be bribed to betray, their trust. Besides the restraints of their personal integrity and honor, the difficulty of acting in concert for purposes of corruption was a security to the public. And if one or a few members only should be seduced, the soundness of the remaining members, would maintain the integrity and fidelity of the body. In the case of the Executive Magistracy which was to be administered by a single man, loss of capacity or corruption was more within the compass of probable events, and either of them might be fatal to the Republic. (p. 128)

The "restraints" of most members of Congress evaporated long ago. Few can boast of any personal integrity or honor. There is no "security to the public" left. Corruption and political ambition have been the rule, not character or any regard for the enumerated powers of Congress cited in the Constitution.

Madison repeatedly, throughout all his writings, insisted that the form of government Americans were adopting must be a *republican* one, not a *democratic* one. A republican government was better advantaged to protect individual rights, while a democracy, regardless of the size of its population, was inherently prone to degenerate into tyranny.

A common passion or interest will, in almost every case, be felt by a majority of the whole; a communication and concert results from the form of government itself; and there is nothing to check the inducements to sacrifice the weaker party, or an obnoxious individual. Hence it is, that such democracies have ever been spectacles of turbulence and contention; have ever been found incompatible with personal security, or the rights of property....Theoretic politicians, who have patronized this species of government, have erroneously supposed, that by reducing mankind to a perfect equality in their political rights, they would, at the same time, be perfectly equalized, and assimilated in their possessions, their opinions, and their passions. (*Federalist* No. 10, p. 164)

Criticisms of the republican form of government were heard from delegates to the Convention and in the press of the time, that it had never been tried before, and so would never work. Madison answered in *Federalist* No. 14, in November 1787:

> Hearken not to the unnatural voice which tells you that the people of America, knit together as they are by so many cords of affection, can no longer live together as members of the same family; can no longer continue the mutual guardians of their mutual happiness; can no longer be fellow citizens of one great respectable and flourishing empire. Hearken not to the voice which petulantly tells you that the form of government recommended for your adoption is a novelty in the political world; that it has never yet had a place in the theories of the wildest projectors; that it rashly attempts what it is impossible to accomplish. (p. 172)

Later in that same number, Madison pays tribute to the genius of the American people:

> But why is the experiment of an extended republic to be rejected merely because it may comprise what is new? Is it not the glory of the people of America, that whilst they have paid a decent regard to the opinions of former times and other nations, they have not suffered a blind veneration for antiquity, for custom, or for names, to overrule the suggestions of their own good sense, the knowledge of their own situation, and the lessons of their own experience? To this manly spirit, posterity will be indebted for the possession, and the world for the example of the numerous innovations displayed on the American theatre, in favour of private rights and public happiness....

> Happily for America, happily we trust for the whole human race, they pursued a new and more noble course. They accomplished a revolution which has no parallel in the annals of human society. (p. 173)

Madison, like many southern delegates to the Convention, was a Virginia slaveholder, and, like Jefferson, Patrick Henry, and others from the region, opposed the institution. But neither he nor they could conceive of a way to end slavery without ruining themselves and precipitating economic and social chaos, and even violent strife. It was proposed during the Convention that the Constitution provide for abolishing slavery in the U.S. by 1808. The idea was opposed inside and outside the Convention because it was perceived to be a violation of property rights. In *Federalist* No. 42, Madison wrote:

> Attempts have been made to pervert this clause into an objection against the constitution, by representing it on one side as a criminal toleration of an illicit practice, and on another, as calculated to prevent voluntary and beneficial emigrations from Europe to America. (p. 237)

Later, Madison spoke before the Virginia Ratifying Convention on the Slave Trade Clause, in June, 1788. He argued in vain for at least a federal or state tax on the slaves brought to American shores, to make the trade economically impractical, and for a total ban by 1808:

> I should conceive this clause to be impolitic, if it were one of those things which could be excluded without encountering greater evils. The southern states would not have entered into the union of America, without the temporary permission of that trade. And if they were excluded from the union, the consequences might be dreadful to them and to us....I need not expatiate on this subject. Great as the evil is, a dismemberment of the union would be worse. (p. 391-392)

Like Jefferson and others who recognized the evil of slavery and of regarding enslaved men as "property," Madison resigned himself to the reluctant consolation that the moral conflict over slavery would need to be resolved by another generation, and possibly violently, and not in his own time.

Citing the great Enlightenment political philosopher, Baron Montesquieu, Madison, in *Federalist* No. 47, reflected on the separation of the executive, legislative, and judicial branches of a republican government:

> The reasons on which Montesquieu grounds his maxim are a further demonstration of his meaning. "When the legislative and executive powers are united in the same person or

body," says he, "there can be no liberty, because apprehensions may arise lest *the same* monarch or senate should *enact* tyrannical laws, to *execute* them in a tyrannical manner." Again, "Were the power of judging joined with the legislative, the life and liberty of the subject would be exposed to arbitrary control, for *the judge* would then be *the legislator*. Were it joined to the executive power, the judge might behave with all the violence of *an oppressor*." (pp. 275-276, emphases Madison's)

Madison was initially ambivalent about a "bill of rights" that would better protect the liberties of Americans. But he eventually warmed to the idea and became one of its most articulate champions. In an October, 1788 letter to Jefferson about what the Constitutional Convention had accomplished and the function of a bill of rights that might be appended to it, in October, he noted:

> ...[T]here are many who think such addition unnecessary, and not a few who think it misplaced in such a Constitution. There is scarce any point on which the part in opposition is so much divided as to its importance and its propriety. My own opinion has always been in favor of a bill of rights; provided it be so framed as not to imply powers not meant to be included in the enumeration. At the same time I have never thought the omission a material defect....

> Wherever the real power in a Government lies, there is the danger of oppression. In our Governments [the federal and state governments] the real power lies in the majority of the Community, and the invasion of private rights is *chiefly* to be apprehended, not from acts of Government contrary to the sense of its constituents, but from acts in which the Government is the mere instrument of the major number of the constituents. (pp. 420-421, emphasis Madison's, square brackets mine)

Finally, Madison realized that no government founded on and dedicated to the preservation of freedom, could be made so tyranny-proof that it would automatically inhibit the rise of tyranny and statism without the conscious, active intervention of men of principle. The integrity of such a government depended wholly on the moral rectitude of men charged with the functions of such a government, men intransigently committed to the proper function and original purpose of such a government. In *Federalist* No. 55, he warns:

> As there is a degree of depravity in mankind which requires a certain degree of circumspection and distrust: So there are other qualities in human nature, which justify a certain portion of esteem and confidence. Republican government presupposes the existence of these qualities in a higher degree than any other form. Were the pictures which have been drawn by the political jealousy of some among us, faithful likenesses of the human character, the inference would be that there is not sufficient virtue among men for self-government; and that nothing less than the chains of despotism can restrain them from destroying and devouring one another. (pp. 319-320)

Obviously, our current lawmakers and ambitious tyrants see Americans as wild beasts that must be restrained by an incrementally imposed despotism. Our electorate has been balkanized into numerous factions that wish to destroy and devour one another, but that is the fault of Congress and every president, Congressman, think tank, and advocacy group that preached victimhood and exemption from the rule of law that was established in the Constitution.

Looking at Madison, and recounting his pearls of wisdom, and remembering that men did exist, though in dwindling numbers from 1788 on who upheld the principles which animated the creation of the Constitution, one feels the sense that one is immersed in a dream-like time of myth and legend.

But, if Madison and the other Founders were the immaterial stuff of legend, if they were truly figments of our imagination, as the swine-like nihilists and deconstructionists claim, none of us would be here today.

James Madison: Writings. Jack N. Rakove, Editor. New York: Library of America, 1999. 966 pp.

March 2014

James Madison
On the Bill of Rights

As a prime mover behind the writing of the Constitution and as a champion of the Bill of Rights, James Madison, as a Representative from Virginia, attended the first sitting of the new Congress in New York and Philadelphia in 1789-1790. While nine of the thirteen states had ratified the Constitution, allowing Congress to hold its first sessions, a strong desire to explicitly secure the freedom won by a long and costly war of independence made appending a bill of rights to the Constitution a first concern of many Americans and critics of the "charter." The absence of such a security in the wording of the Constitution and from the enumerated powers of the federal government did not assure the document's critics that life, liberty and the pursuit of happiness were adequately protected from abuses of power.

What the critics saw was a document which detailed the limitations of federal government power (the enumerations), but no written assurances that, should individuals in that government overstep or abuse their powers, they could be opposed and charged with tyranny or corruption in the pursuit unlimited power. Defenders of the Constitution dismissed these concerns, saying, on one hand, that their absence from the document was instead an assurance of their inviolability; and, on the other hand, that a "bill of rights" questioned the legitimacy of any powers granted to the federal government in its enumerated powers (and, by implication, a questioning of the legitimate powers of the state governments), or would leave other, unnamed rights open to violation and government mischief.

The call for a "bill of rights" to be incorporated into the federal constitution was inspired by the Virginia Declaration of Rights, adopted in the summer of 1776 before the proclamation of the Declaration of Independence. George Mason was its principal author. As noted in "Pearls of James Madison, Founder," Madison was originally dubious about the value and function of a bill of rights in the federal scheme of things, but eventually saw their necessity and carried the fight for a bill of rights to the Congress's deliberations on a host of post-ratification matters. As did George Mason. The Constitution Society noted:

> As passed, the Virginia Declaration was largely the work of
> George Mason; the committee and the Convention made

some verbal changes and added Sections 10 and 14. This declaration served as a model for bills of rights in several other state constitutions and was a source of the French Declaration of the Rights of Man and of the Citizen, though its degree of influence upon the latter document is a highly controversial question. The reference to "property" in Section I may be compared with the use of the word by John Locke, its omission by Thomas Jefferson from the second paragraph of the Declaration of Independence, and its use in the Constitution, Amendments V and XIV.

George Mason (1725-92), one of Virginia's wealthiest planters, a neighbor and friend of Washington, is best remembered for his part in drafting the Virginia constitution of 1776. In 1787 he was a leader in the Federal Convention. Refusing to sign the completed document, Mason, along with Patrick Henry and others, opposed its ratification in the Virginia Convention of 1788.]

As noted in my original column, the term *property* was omitted from the Declaration because of the slavery issue. To recruit the southern colonies in a united Declaration, the term was omitted from the final draft insofar as it meant involuntary human bondage as a legitimate form of property. Jefferson, a lifelong opponent of slavery, was as helpless in the circumstances as any other critic of the institution:

Jefferson wrote that slavery was like holding "a wolf by the ear, and we can neither hold him, nor safely let him go." He thought that his cherished federal union, the world's first democratic experiment, would be destroyed by slavery. To emancipate slaves on American soil, Jefferson thought, would result in a large-scale race war that would be as brutal and deadly as the slave revolt in Haiti in 1791. But he also believed that to keep slaves in bondage, with part of America in favor of abolition and part of America in favor of perpetuating slavery, could only result in a civil war that would destroy the union. Jefferson's latter prediction was correct: in 1861, the contest over slavery sparked a bloody civil war and the creation of two nations—Union and Confederacy—in the place of one.

Like Jefferson and others who recognized the evil of slavery and of regarding enslaved men as "property," Madison resigned himself to the reluctant consolation that the moral conflict over slavery would need to be resolved by another generation, and possibly violently, and not in his own time.

Patrick Henry, the most famous and articulate opponent of ratification of the Constitution (an "Anti-Federalist"), warned the Virginia Convention that it should at least insist that the new Congress take up the issue of a bill of rights. In his 24th and last speech during the Convention before it adjourned, he said:

> Mr. Chairman, when we were told of the difficulty of obtaining previous amendments, I contended that they might be as easily obtained as subsequent amendments. We are told that nine states have adopted it. If so, when the government gets in motion, have they not a right to consider our amendments as well as if we adopted first? If we remonstrate, may they not consider and admit our amendments?

> But now, sir, when we have been favored with a view of their subsequent amendments, I am confirmed in what I apprehended; and that is, subsequent amendments will make our condition worse; for they are placed in such a point of view as will make this Convention ridiculous. I speak in plain, direct language. It is extorted from me. If this Convention will say, that the very right by which amendments are desired is not secured, then I say our rights are not secured. As we have the right of desiring amendments, why not exercise it? But gentlemen deny this right, it follows, of course, that, if this right be not secured, our other fights are not.

> The proposition of subsequent amendments {650} is only to lull our apprehensions. We speak the language of contradiction and inconsistency, to say that rights are secured, and then say that they are not. Is not this placing this Convention in a contemptible light? Will not this produce contempt of us in Congress, and every other part of

the world? Will gentlemen tell me that they are in earnest about these amendments?

On June 8th, 1789, Madison spoke about the dissatisfaction with the Constitution not even exhibiting in its entirety a token security of liberty. All quotations of Madison here are from *James Madison: Writings*.*

> It cannot be a secret to the gentlemen in this house, that, notwithstanding the ratification of this system of government by eleven of the thirteen United States, in some cases unanimously, in others by large majorities; yet still there is a great number of our constituents who are dissatisfied with it; among whom are many respectable for their talents, their patriotism, and respectable for the jealousy they have for their liberty, which, thought mistaken in its object, is laudable in its motive. There is a great body of people falling under this description....

> We ought not to disregard their inclination, but, on principles of amity and moderation, conform to their wishes, and expressly declare the great rights of mankind secured under this constitution. (p. 439)

Discussing in their embryonic form some of the amendments to be taken up by the House, Madison outlined them for his colleagues:

> That the people have an indubitable, unalienable, and indefeasible right to reform or change their government, whenever it be found adverse or inadequate to the purposes of its institution....

> The civil rights of none shall be abridged on account of religious belief or worship, nor shall any national religion be established, nor shall the full and equal rights of conscience be in any manner, or on any pretext infringed.

> The people shall not be deprived or abridged of their right to speak, to write, or to publish their sentiments; and the freedom of the press, as one of the great bulwarks of liberty, shall be inviolable.

The people shall not be restrained from peaceably assembling and consulting for their common good; nor from applying to the legislature by petitions, or remonstrances for redress of their grievances.

The right of the people to keep and bear arms shall not be infringed; a well armed, and well regulated militia being the best security of a free country: but no person religiously scrupulous of bearing arms, shall be compelled to render military service in person. (pp. 442-443)

Madison went on to itemize the proposed amendments covering the prohibition against double jeopardy, bearing witness against oneself, excessive bail, cruel and unusual punishments, the right to due process, and the prohibition of seizure of private property without just compensation.

The rights of the people to be secured in their persons, their houses, their papers, and their other property from all unreasonable searches and seizures, shall not be violated by warrants issued without probable cause, supported by oath or affirmation, or not particularly describing the places to be searched, or the persons or things to be seized.

In all criminal prosecutions, the accused shall enjoy the right to a speedy trial, to be informed of the cause and nature of the accusation. To be confronted with his accusers, and the witnesses against him; to have a compulsory process for obtaining witnesses in his favor; and to have the assistance of counsel for his defense. (p. 443)

Not forgetting the states and their relationship with the federal government, Madison added:

No state shall violate the rights of conscience, or the freedom of the press, or the trial by jury in criminal cases. (p. 443)

And, finally:

> The powers not delegated by this constitution, nor prohibited by it to the states, are reserved to the States respectively. (p. 444)

Answering the imagined dangers of a bill of rights argued by others, Madison discoursed to the assembly on the benefits of having a bill of rights, and how the absence of one affected the governance of other nations, especially Great Britain.

> I acknowledge the ingenuity of those arguments which were drawn against the constitution, by a comparison with the policy of Great-Britain, in establishing a declaration of rights; but there is too great of difference in the case to warrant the comparison; therefore the arguments drawn from that source, were in a great measure inapplicable. In the declaration of rights which that country has established, the truth is, they have gone no farther, than to raise a barrier against the power of the crown; the power of the legislature is left altogether indefinite.

> Although I know whenever the great rights, the trial by jury, freedom of the press, or liberty of conscience, came in question in that body, the invasion of them is resisted by able advocates, yet their Magna Charta does not contain any one provision for the security of those rights, respecting which, the people of America are most alarmed. The freedom of the press and the rights of conscience, those choicest privileges of the people, are unguarded in the British constitution. (p. 445)

Madison, of course, could not have foreseen the "imperial" presidencies of men like Franklin D. Roosevelt and Barack Obama, whose executive actions have trumped the function of Congress (too often with its acquiescence), and, indeed, would not recognize the federal government as it exists today, a wealth-consuming and rights-negating behemoth which has usurped Americans' rights and shredded the Constitution.

> In our government it is, perhaps, less necessary to guard against the abuse of the executive department than any other; because it is not the stronger branch of the system, but the weaker. It therefore must be levelled against the legislative,

for it is the most powerful, and most likely to be abused, because it is under the least control; hence, so far as a declaration of rights can tend to prevent the exercise of undue power, it cannot be doubted but such a declaration is proper. (p. 446)

Madison prefaces his concerns that even a government whose powers have been enumerated in favor of protecting liberty from "off the books" tyranny or arbitrary power exercised through loopholes in wording or content has serious shortcomings. He leads up to the power of taxation:

It is true the powers of the general government are circumscribed; they are directed to particular objects; but even if government keeps within those limits, it has certain discretionary powers with respect to the means, which may admit of abuse to a certain extent, in the same manner as the powers of the state governments under their constitutions may to an indefinite extent; because in the constitution of the United States there is a clause granting to Congress the power to make all laws which are necessary and proper for carrying into execution the powers vested in the government of the United States....

The general government has a right to pass all laws which shall be necessary to collect its revenue; the means for enforcing the collection are within the direction of the legislature: may not general warrants be considered necessary for this purpose?...If there was reason for restraining the state governments from exercising this power, there is like reason for restraining the federal government. (pp. 447-448)

Taxation, in Madison's time (and, indeed, throughout history) was the only "necessary and proper" way men thought a government could raise money to perform even its legitimate functions, such as maintaining the courts, maintaining an armed force to stave off invasion, and maintaining a civil police force. But even the most ardent and ambitious statists in Madison's generation (such as Alexander Hamilton) would have found unimaginable a government which presumed it "necessary and proper" to protect the environment, provide subsidized housing, subsidize food purchases, police the securities business, monopolize education, regulate nutrition, provide pensions and medical care subsidies, enforce the purchase of medical insurance, subsidize medical and scientific research, and etc., and also to debase its own currency to pay for these things in an ever-widening range of powers.

The term *necessary and proper* has been interpreted by lawmakers and courts over the last two centuries to cover every possible "crisis" the government feels committed to regulate and able to police and resolve. If you are not a smoker, the government thinks it "necessary and proper" to protect you against smokers. If you are obese, the government thinks it "necessary and proper" to impose a nutrition regimen. If you are a student, the government thinks it "necessary and proper" to teach you. If you are "poor," the government thinks it "necessary and proper" to support you in a variety of economic ways. If you are a member of a designated "minority," the government thinks it "necessary and proper" to protect you from discrimination.

One could list a hundred-page list in tiny print of human relations and actions the government thinks it "necessary and proper" to legislate for and has the "inherent" power to act on. This is not freedom as Madison and his contemporaries imagined it. It is a clanking web of chains and fetters on your limbs and on your mind.

What has happened is that state governments – and even municipal ones – have simply emulated the federal government in assuming illegitimate powers of taxation and control of virtually every aspect of an individual's life and actions in the course of pursuing his happiness.

We also have in effect through the federal government bills of attainder and ex post facto laws, which are expressly forbidden in Article I, Section 10, Clause 1. Wealthy individuals in the public eye have been targeted by the government to make examples of (e.g., Michael Miliken, Leona Helmsley, even Redd Foxx) to frighten the public into obedience in terms of *ex officio* bills of attainder issued by the SEC, the IRS, the Justice Department, and even the EPA.

An example of an undeclared ex post facto law was the arrest and imprisonment of Nakoula Basseley Nakoula, maker of the "Innocence of Muslims" YouTube trailer, on the unsubstantiated assertion (and later exposed as a "What difference does it make?" lie) of Secretary of State Hillary Clinton that the trailer was responsible for the Benghazi attacks.

The unwritten law is that it is illegal to make films that purportedly and potentially would incite "justifiable" violence by Muslims by "disrespecting" or blaspheming against Islam or any of its icons or tenets.

In conclusion, America is as far away from the original intent of the Bill of Rights as it is from the original purpose of the original Constitution, subsequently amended in 1913 to include the 16th and 17th Amendments establishing a pernicious income tax and the direct, popular election of U.S. senators.

To the Marxists, socialists, liberals, and other statists who reside in the bubble world of Progressivism, this is indeed "progress" *away* from life, liberty, and the pursuit of happiness, to a condition of stasis, security, and institutionalized selflessness.

**James Madison: Writings*. Jack N. Rakove, Editor. New York: Library of America, 1999. 966 pp.

March 2014

What's to Like About JFK?

This rhetorical question could just as easily be rephrased to elicit the same answers: What's *not* to like about JFK?

Plenty.

Most of the commentary I read on the 50th anniversary of President John F. Kennedy's assassination on November 22nd 1963 exuded a special, repulsive kind of adulation, combined with almost tearful reminiscences of what the country was like half a century ago (it was a *bad* country, ready to be knocked into shape by a great leader) and plaintive projections of what it could have been had JFK been allowed to complete his presumably first term in office (it would have been a *good* country, able to take its place among the best welfare states in the world).

The joke is on the sigh-filled dreamers. We have in President Barack Obama's two terms almost precisely what JFK would have created: a semi-socialist, semi-fascist government dedicated to "leading" the country to "greater" things, an administration determined to marshal Americans to march in lockstep in the direction the White House and its allies in Congress wish us to go, complete with a "charismatic" icon of a leader, glib of tongue and murky in his motives.

Much of the commentary was so maudlin that it caused one to wonder about the mental health of the individuals who wrote it. For example, the New York Times chose to reprint humorist Art Buchwald's New York Herald Tribune poem, "We Weep," from November 26, 1963:

> We weep for our President who died for his country.
> We weep for his wife and for his children.
> We weep for his mother and father and brothers and sisters.
> We weep for the millions of people who are weeping for him.
> We weep for Americans, that this could happen in our country.
>
> We weep for the Europeans.
> And the Africans.
> And the Asians.

And people in every corner of the globe who saw in him a
hope for the future and a chance for mankind.
We weep for our children and their children and everyone's
children.
For he was charting their destinies as he was charting ours.
We weep for the Negro who saw in him a chance for a
decent life.

And etc.

Had enough? There are two more stanzas, just as bad, but I thought you
should be spared them. Kathleen Parker of the Washington Post, in her
November 22nd "A Tribute to John F. Kennedy," picks up Buchwald's
lachrymose sentiment fifty years later, but adds something revealing about
herself and how she perceived the country in November 1963:

> …Neither the truth nor the myth of the man seems to matter
> as much as the deeply personal experience of hearing the
> words:

> "President Kennedy is dead."

> "A death in the family" is how many have described that
> day, and this is as accurate as any explanation, especially for
> people who were children then. The president and Mrs.
> Kennedy were more than the nation's first family; they were
> our parents, too. We identified with the children and looked
> up to the grown-ups.…

> Thus, when Kennedy died, we lost our symbolic father and
> our grief was for ourselves as well as the Kennedys.…

If truth be told, when I learned of JFK's death, I felt nothing. As a high
school senior, I'd felt nothing but an irritation with the man, coupled with
a sense of impending doom, which I was able to identify only years later.
Listening to his speeches grated against my aural sensibilities; it was like
hearing someone run his fingernails down a blackboard. I'd watched film
clips of Adolf Hitler and Benito Mussolini haranguing rapt crowds on
television, and JFK gave me that same feeling, that he was an ominous
threat to my life and to my future, and that if I stood in the way of the

leagues of admiring, emotion-driven mobs, I'd simply be trampled to death.

This was not a pretty or flattering observation to make about "my fellow Americans."

But I never then nor have I ever regarded JFK or Jackie Kennedy as "parents" to "look up to." I did not want a "leader," did not want to be lead, did not want to be "taken care of," did not want to be immersed in some hideous, identity-erasing *gestalt* of national purpose. The notion of "belonging" to a collective was an alien and repellant one.

In fact, I grew to despise the whole Kennedy clan, from Joe Kennedy, Senior, who made his initial fortune as a bootlegger, clear up to Ted Kennedy, whose political career should have been aborted because of Chappaquiddick, Mary Jo Kopechne, and the charge of homicide that was never levied against him, but in whose name and memory ObamaCare was largely passed, and all of JFK's children. The whole spoiled, power-lusting bunch of them.

I despised the JFK "Camelot" myth as much as I mistrusted the whole FDR myth, because it was the unreserved canonization of these two political figures which caused me to smell something rotten in Denmark.

I subscribe to a number of "pro-freedom" weblogs. Some of these organizations are scarier than any George Soros Progressive organizations. Liberty Counsel, which touts the line that the U.S. is founded on Biblical principles, is one of those. I received this "alert" just this morning:

> Yesterday, as a nation, we commemorated the 50th anniversary of the assassination of President John F. Kennedy. The words most associated with JFK came from his 1961 Inaugural Address, "My fellow Americans, ask not what your country can do for you. Ask what you can do for your country." It's not hard to see how far "progressive" liberalism has taken our nation away from this simple patriotic proclamation in 50 years and how foreign that concept is to the current administration.

Religious American conservatives are not the only ones smitten with JFK. Europe doesn't seem to have lost its ardor for him. For example, here are the words of a Briton, Sean Collins, Spiked's American correspondent, on the 50th anniversary:

> ...Most of all, Kennedy injected a sense of dynamism and optimism into politics, and people were willing to believe in him. He encouraged public activism and responsibility, in his call 'ask not what your country can do for you, ask what you can do for your country'. He aimed high, urging a manned flight to the moon before the end of the decade (even though the technology to do so was hardly evident). Americans were problem-solvers, and there were few limits to what could be achieved - that was his message.

> JFK came to symbolise optimism and idealism (even if he didn't ultimately live up to it), and his assassination appeared to be the death, not just of the man, but of what he symbolised. People hoped Kennedy would bring a new era of prosperity and innovation; but as the years passed, his assassination appeared to mark the beginning of an era of decline. Reagan, Clinton and Obama attempted to reintroduce optimism into American politics, but all paled in comparison with the genuine optimism that greeted JFK, and all ultimately proved to be let-downs.

In many ways, not a few of them scandalous, JFK served as a "role model" for another destroyer of the country, Bill Clinton. One thing that anchored the political philosophy connection between Clinton and JFK was the startling, full-page photograph of 16-year-old Bill Clinton shaking hands with JFK in the White House Rose Garden. I think I saw it in the New York Times, and have that page buried somewhere in my archives. I dubbed it, "Passing the Torch." A video was made of the encounter. That photograph, however, concretized what I had observed was the perilous direction the country was taking.

I left this comment on a November 22nd FrontPage article, "Fact, Democrats, and the JFK Legend," by Bruce Thornton, who debunks JFK's legislative record:

JFK was a fascist. Any president or president-elect who asks Americans what "they can do for their country" is simply emulating what Hitler asked of Germans and Mussolini asked of Italians. "I'll cut taxes and shake my fist at the Commies, but you have to follow me and live for the country, not for yourself." Compared to current Democrats and Progressives, JFK looks squeaky clean, almost nostalgic. But he was still bad news. If he'd said in public that the government should get out of the economy and out of education, I'd cut him some slack. But, like his fellow Democrats, he just assumed that the government had a mission to run the economy and educate Americans. He was a statist, and a fascist to boot.

No one today dares call JFK a fascist. But his style, his rhetoric, and his behavior all comport with the means and ends of fascism. JFK, on a European tour before he entered politics, expressed admiration for the Nazis. Only last May, in a book review by Alan Hall in the British <u>Daily Mail</u>, it was revealed that JFK wrote in his journal:

'Fascism?' wrote the youthful president-to-be in one. 'The right thing for Germany.' In another; 'What are the evils of fascism compared to communism?'

And on August 21, 1937 - two years before the war that would claim 50 million lives broke out - he wrote: 'The Germans really are too good - therefore people have ganged up on them to protect themselves.'

And in a line which seems directly plugged into the racial superiority line plugged by the Third Reich he wrote after travelling through the Rhineland: 'The Nordic races certainly seem to be superior to the Romans.'

Other musings concern how great the autobahns were - 'the best roads in the world' - and how, having visited Hitler's Bavarian holiday home in Berchtesgaden and the tea house built on top of the mountain for him. He declared; 'Who has visited these two places can easily imagine how Hitler will emerge from the hatred currently surrounding him to emerge in a few years as one of the most important personalities that ever lived.'

Liberal columnist Dylan Matthews, in his November 22nd Washington Post opinion piece, "Americans think John F. Kennedy was one of our greatest presidents. He wasn't," credits Lyndon Johnson with accomplishing what JFK set out to do but was assassinated before he could realize his legislative goals.

Conservative George Will, however, claims JFK was a "conservative." In his November 20th Washington Post column, "The JFK we had and the memory that lives," he wrote:

> ...Many who call him difficult to understand seem eager to not understand him. They present as puzzling or uncharacteristic aspects of his politics about which he was consistent and unambiguous. For them, his conservative dimension is an inconvenient truth. Ira Stoll, in "JFK, Conservative," tries to prove too much but assembles sufficient evidence that his book's title is not merely provocative.
>
> A Look magazine headline in June 1946 read: "A Kennedy Runs for Congress: The Boston-bred scion of a former ambassador is a fighting-Irish conservative." Neither his Cold War anti-communism, which was congruent with President Harry Truman's, nor his fiscal conservatism changed dramatically during his remaining 17 years.

It was left to his successor in office, Lyndon B. Johnson, to create the massive welfare state which JFK was sure to have pushed for himself, given his pragmatic way of finding things for government to do and purposes for Americans to hove to, to win brownie points with an mesmerized public and a forgiving news media. Rand Simberg, in his November 22nd USA TODAYcolumn, "Dear NASA: President Kennedy just wasn't that into you," casts credible doubts on JFK's commitment to an American space program, calling NASA a "centralized state-socialist bureaucracy that we established to beat the Soviets' state-socialist bureaucracy to the moon."

Larry Sabato in his November 20th Washington Post column, "Lead like John F. Kennedy," lists JFK's strong and weak points. Among the strong points was his way with words and not needing an electronic cue card/teleprompter to deliver speeches, as does the current specimen in office:

> Kennedy hired a superb wordsmith, Ted Sorensen, who substantially wrote JFK's book "Profiles in Courage," his stirring inaugural address and many other well-known speeches. Yet Kennedy was no parrot. He was a marvelous editor and wordsmith, too, and he could talk extemporaneously without a text for long stretches.

Sorensen wrote JFK's signature statement: "And so, my fellow Americans, ask not what your country can do for you, ask what you can do for your country." Or apparently it was plagiarized (by Sorensen and JFK in a "collaborative" composition of the inaugural address of January 20th 1961) from an oft-repeated homily by JFK's headmaster at the elite Choate School, according to a November 1st, 2011 book review by the Daily Mail of Chris "Tingle" Matthews' *Jack Kennedy: Elusive Hero*.

> U.S. author Chris Matthews makes the claims in *Jack Kennedy: Elusive Hero*. He unearthed notes written by George St John, the President's former headmaster at Choate School in Connecticut, which suggest he had been aware of the 'ask not' line for many years.

> The papers quote a Harvard College dean's refrain: 'As has often been said, the youth who loves his Alma Mater will always ask not "what can she do for me?" but "what can I do for her?"'

And Matthews is an admirer of Kennedy, not motivated to smear or denigrate JFK.

But whether or not the inaugural address line was plagiarized, it deserves parsing. What JFK said before speaking that line is important to take into context. He was, with very little ambiguity, asking Americans and the country to devote themselves to "saving" the world for "freedom," although what he meant by "freedom" is lost in an ambiguity deliberately calculated to appeal to emotions, not reason. He was sanctioning the federal government's taking the lead in that "selfless" campaign in "a struggle against the common enemies of man: tyranny, poverty, disease, and war itself." This echoes Wilsonian Progressivism, which called for the U.S. to become the supreme global exemplar of selfless service to "noble causes." This is unadulterated altruism.

Much of the inaugural address was written as an answer to the Soviet Union. Nowhere in it does JFK hint at what Americans were asking their country (or him) to do for them. Doubtless, JFK was not asking Americans to fight for their country by championing individual rights, the sanctity of private property, and freedom of speech. Far from it. *Liberty* was the last thing on his mind.

But the person who nailed JFK's politics and warned of the dangers he represented to the country was novelist/philosopher Ayn Rand, long before he was assassinated, long before anyone else began to smell something rotten in Washington D.C.

In her provocative column, "The Fascist New Frontier," based on an address she gave at Ford Hall Forum in Boston in 1962, she wrote:

> The difference between [socialism and fascism] is superficial and purely formal, but it is significant psychologically: it brings the authoritarian nature of a planned economy crudely into the open.... [p. 98]

> Under fascism, citizens retain the responsibilities of owning property, without freedom to act and without any of the advantages of ownership. Under socialism, government officials acquire all the advantages of ownership, without any of the responsibilities, since they do not hold title to the property, but merely the right to use it—at least until the next purge. In either case, the government officials hold the economic, political and legal power of life or death over the citizens.....[p. 98]

> Under both systems, sacrifice is invoked as a magic, omnipotent solution in any crisis—and "the public good" is the altar on which victims are immolated. But there are stylistic differences of emphasis. The socialist-communist axis keeps promising to achieve abundance, material comfort

and security for its victims, in some indeterminate future. The fascist-Nazi axis scorns material comfort and security, and keeps extolling some undefined sort of spiritual duty, service and conquest. [p. 106]

But, surely, freedom of speech would be guaranteed under a fascist régime, wouldn't it?. Quite the contrary, wrote Rand.

Freedom of speech means freedom from interference, suppression or punitive action by the government—and nothing else. It does not mean the right to demand the financial support or the material means to express your views at the expense of other men who may not wish to support you. Freedom of speech includes the freedom not to agree, not to listen and not to support one's own antagonists. A "right" does not include the material implementation of that right by other men; it includes only the freedom to earn that implementation by one's own effort. Private citizens cannot use physical force or coercion; they cannot *censor* or *suppress* anyone's views or publications. Only the government can do so. And *censorship* is a concept that pertains *only* to governmental action. [p. 106]

By what means could the government establish censorship without scaring men off, without *calling it* censorship? By pressure applied by the myriad federal agencies that regulate business and men's actions in the private sphere of our "mixed economy." Rand wrote:

The dividing line – the *frontier* – between a "mixed economy" and a dictatorship lies in the issue of freedom of speech; the establishment of censorship is the tombstone of a free country. Observe the concerted efforts of the administration to push – or rather, to smuggle – us across *that* particular frontier. I say "to smuggle," because these efforts are as devious as the New Frontiersmen's use of language – and the fog of their terminology is here at its thickest....[pp. 105-106]

...Rule by hidden, unprovable intimidation relies on the victims' "voluntary" self-enslavement. The result is worse than a censored press: it is a servile press. [p. 109]

And what have we had for at least the last half century but a servile, boot-licking press that cheers on any candidate who preaches "volunteerism" and "wealth redistribution" and deference to the "public good" and all the other collectivist panaceas?

Barack Hussein Obama was only a year old when Rand wrote those words. But they apply to him and his administration as well as to JFK and his administration. And I think, tough as she was, she would have swooned in disbelief at the state of a country that would elect the likes of Obama – twice. (She died in 1982.)

What's to like about JFK?

I would say: *Nothing.*

*"The Fascist New Frontier," by Ayn Rand, in *The Ayn Rand Column*. Ed. Peter Schwartz. Irvine CA: Ayn Rand Institute Press, 1998.

November 2013

Charting Our Destinies: From FDR to Obama

In "What's to Like About JFK?" I cited humorist Art Buchwald's maudlin poem about the assassination of John F. Kennedy in Dallas on November 22nd, 1963, as an example of how captivated Americans were by JFK. Two lines from the second stanza stuck in my mind:

> We weep for our children and their children and everyone's children. For he was charting their destinies as he was charting ours…..etc.

And so were Lyndon B. Johnson, Richard Nixon, Jimmy Carter, Ronald Reagan, George Bushes I and II, Bill Clinton, and Barack Obama.

Did any American ask them to? No. Like John F. Kennedy, they, too, just assumed it was the proper function of government to establish national "goals" and the natural role of the office of president to "lead" us to them. To chart our destinies.

But, where to? What were those goals? What precisely was the nature of the *destination*?

The problem I've had with virtually every presidential address I've ever heard or read and that was made in the 20th and 21st centuries, aside from their content, is that they've been fundamentally authoritarian in nature. "I'm here to lead, and this is where we are going, or ought to go. No kicking and screaming, please, there's a good fellow." The presumptive role of presidential "leadership" has always been abrasive to my sense of having a choice in my own destiny, and not that of anyone else's, and especially not the plans of a "leader." I don't want someone, and especially not the government, "charting" my destiny.

Few questioned the propriety of a president setting himself up as a kind of executive Scout Master prepared to lead his Cubs on a non-stop crusade to "do good." Too many Americans were susceptible to JFK's emotion-appealing rhetoric and felt a zing in their hearts when he turned on the charm, donned the mantel of "leadership," and began pointing in a multitude of directions.

On March 9, 2007, the late Ted Sorensen, JFK's principal speechwriter, special counsel and adviser, endorsed Obama for president in 2007, worked in Obama's 2008 campaign, and even provided assistance on Obama's inaugural address. Sorensen claimed that he and JFK collaborated closely on speeches. But Sorensen, a liberal, would not have written anything that JFK would have had reservations saying in public; however, JFK would not have much disagreed with anything Sorensen wrote.

Sorensen says, in this video, comparing JFK with Barack Obama, that Obama, among other things,

> "...has that same spirit, that same desire, to call to public service, especially the young people, all the citizens of this country, to live up to that great title, 'American citizen.'"

When Sorensen died in October 2010, the Associated Press published an effusive obituary that all but canonized the speechwriter, as well. Sorensen's career with JFK began in 1956.

> Of the courtiers to Camelot's king, special counsel Sorensen ranked just below Kennedy's brother Bobby. He was the adoring, tireless speechwriter and confidant to a president whose term was marked by Cold War struggles, growing civil rights strife and the beginnings of the U.S. intervention in Vietnam.

> Some of Kennedy's most memorable speeches, from his inaugural address to his vow to place a man on the moon, resulted from such close collaborations with Sorensen that scholars debated who wrote what. He had long been suspected as the real writer of the future president's Pulitzer Prize-winning "Profiles in Courage," an allegation Sorensen and the Kennedys emphatically - and litigiously - denied.

In short, what "they can do for their country." Except that, in Obama's case, it is an issue of what he is *doing to it*.

Brian Marquard, in his November 1st, 2010 Boston Globe article on Sorensen's death, wrote:

"I think Ted became the most important adviser and, on balance, I think he was the best of the brightest and best," said Harris Wofford, a former US senator from Pennsylvania who had served as an adviser to Kennedy. "He also knew what John Ken nedy thought. They had an extraordinary relationship. It would be hard to know where one person's thoughts ended and the other began."

Officially, Mr. Sorensen was special counsel to the president, a role he reprised with Lyndon B. Johnson. Mr. Sorensen worked so closely with Jack Kennedy, however, that he became widely regarded as the president's alter ego, liberal conscience, and intellectual confidant. Kennedy sought Mr. Sorensen's counsel at every key juncture, from campaigning for the White House to guiding the country through perilous times such as the Bay of Pigs invasion and the Cuban missile crisis.

By Mr. Sorensen's description, the two were as one as they drafted turns of phrase Kennedy made famous. Scholars in decades since have parsed sentences and scoured records while trying to deduce who wrote which words.

A number of conservative weblogs and online news outlets have paid compliments to President John F. Kennedy's vaunted anti-communism and virtually enshrined him in the pantheon of American leaders and presidents, simply because of his hostility to the Soviet Union.

JFK's friendliness with the welfare state is ignored by them. Had he lived to have a second term in office, doubtless he would have accomplished at least half what Lyndon B. Johnson, his successor in office after his assassination, accomplished in establishing a full-scale welfare state.

Nowhere in his speeches as a senator from Massachusetts, as a presidential candidate, and as president is there any indication that he was opposed to welfare state legislation. Sorensen, the son of a progressive liberal politician, was one, as well. He and JFK could not have worked so effectively together had there been a fundamental difference in their political thinking. One was Tweedledum, the other Tweedledee.

Out of the 2,256-word Dallas speech (almost twice as long as JFK's inaugural address), the term *freedom* occurs eleven times, while *leadership* occurs eight times. For what is *leadership* leading to? What would JFK's goals have been? No one seems to have ever questioned his role as a "leader," but what would he have led us to? The phrase from Art Buchwald's tearful "We Weep" poem from November 1963, "charting our destinies," bothered me, because it is the antithesis of freedom. The presumption needed to be challenged.

The undertone of the Dallas speech, which focuses on America's military deterrence capabilities, is off-putting because it communicates something other than a concern for the country's safety and survival. That undertone is: The country is mine to manage and to set in the right direction (whatever direction that might be, which is certainly, given JFK's liberal credentials, *not* in the direction of freedom), and I expect you to do your part.

None of the steps discussed by JFK in his undelivered speech would have been necessary had President Franklin D. Roosevelt been receptive to invading Europe through the Balkans, as Churchill had advocated in order to cut off the Red Army (before it had even broken out of Russia), to securing a surrender of the Nazi government in return for joining an Allied effort to oppose Stalin and his designs on Eastern Europe (a surrender German generals had sent unacknowledged feelers to Roosevelt about), or even to giving aid and succor to the very real anti-Nazi underground in Germany, an underground which reached into the highest ranks of the Wehrmacht.

For a first-class discussion and detailed revelation of the disgraceful roots of the "Cold War" and the role of Soviet espionage, of the Soviet penetration of FDR's administration, and of the treason of fellow-traveling Americans in the government during his years in office, see Diana West's *American Betrayal: The Secret Assault on Our Nation's Character*, a work reviled by Leftists and Neocons alike because it departs from, challenges, and exposes the standard estimate of FDR and the conduct of WWII. See also her *The Rebuttal: Defending 'American Betrayal' from the Book-Burners*, in which she counters every criticism of *American Betrayal* and exposes her virulent, smear-happy critics as ambitious censors. The West could have been spared the cost in lives and treasure of the "Cold War" had the Soviet Union been allowed to collapse during or shortly after WWII. Here is tantalizing excerpt from *American Betrayal*, recreating an event that occurred in Washington D.C. in the summer of 1941:

> ...It's a good bet State Department office windows were open in those pre-air-conditioning days. Maybe a passerby heard the percussive beats of a manual typewriter as Loy Henderson, a resolutely anti-Communist Foreign Service officer, tapped out a plan for the United States in the increasingly likely, even expected event that Hitler's Germany attacked Stalin's Russia somewhere along a line of battle four or five thousand miles away from Foggy Bottom – as indeed the Germans would do in launching "Barbarossa" the very next day. It was June 21, 1941.

> ...Finally, *should the Soviet régime fall...the sky won't fall, too*. This is a cloud-parting concept, revealing beacons of a never-before-glimpsed light. *Finally, should the Soviet régime fall...we should let it. Finally, should the Soviet régime fall...an anti-Communist government could take its place after the war....*[pp. 244-245, *American Betrayal*]

Instead, the Soviet régime was propped up by FDR's policies, not least of which was the cornucopia of benefits from Lend Lease, which enabled the Soviets to resist the Nazi invasion, and later to swallow Eastern Europe, replacing Nazi tyranny with Soviet tyranny.

As with his inaugural address in January 1961, the main thrust of JFK's Dallas speech was anti-communist and pro-defense, emphasizing the importance of nuclear deterrence. Still, the Dallas speech echoes a call to arms in the way of committing the country to the defense of freedom. Yet the problem is that JFK never really burdened himself or his rhetoric with a *definition* of freedom. He used it in a general, insinuative sense, counting on his auditors to fill in the blanks about what freedom is or what it meant to them, basing their understanding of what JFK might have meant by it in an unspoken consensus of what I have described elsewhere of calculated ambiguity.

And his message always was: You exist and have some freedom to make America great, but for no other reason, and I'll decide whether or not you're worthy of praise.

By way of comparison, reading President-elect <u>Calvin Coolidge</u>'s inaugural speech of March 1925, one doesn't get the sense that Coolidge is taking charge of everyone's life, or assuming command of the country's destiny. He had no charisma and certainly wasn't photogenic. He was neither a glad-hander nor a philandering playboy as were most of the Kennedy men. <u>Listening</u> to him read on the radio from a script on the "Duty of Government" doesn't give one the impression, either, that he was a man on a white horse ready to save the nation. His principle message to Americans was that the future of the nation as a free country was up to them, not him.

Coolidge's addresses, in print and on radio, contain a mixture of virtues and fatal flaws, but one doesn't get the sense, either, that he ever talked down to Americans. He did not see himself as a member of some elite group prepared to lead the country out of a desert. The <u>White House page</u> on Coolidge reports:

> In his Inaugural he asserted that the country had achieved "a state of contentment seldom before seen," and pledged himself to maintain the status quo. In subsequent years he twice vetoed farm relief bills, and killed a plan to produce cheap Federal electric power on the Tennessee River.
>
> The political genius of President Coolidge, Walter Lippmann pointed out in 1926, was his talent for effectively doing nothing: "This active inactivity suits the mood and certain of the needs of the country admirably. It suits all the business interests which want to be let alone.... And it suits all those who have become convinced that government in this country has become dangerously complicated and top-heavy...."

JFK uttering the word "freedom" meant nothing to him or to Sorensen, and this is clear when one examines their shared political philosophy, because they never define the term. Uttering the word cost JFK nothing. He had fascist designs on the country. He asked Americans what "<u>they can do for their country</u>," and this exhortation echoed Hitler's and Mussolini's asking Germans and Italians what "they could do for their countries." They were demanding that the citizens of those countries recalibrate their lives to live for the sake and glory of the race or the nation.

Remember that Hitler and Mussolini both were anti-communist, and continually fulminated against the Communists, not because they abhorred Communism, but because it was a competing totalitarian ideology, a rival statist political philosophy. JFK asked Americans to recalibrate their lives, too. JFK was a political pragmatist looking for something to do, something to be a "leader" of, but it had to be a collectivist or altruist cause. He was as much a welfare statist as was LBJ and his successors, including Ronald Reagan, but most especially Bill and Hillary Clinton, both Bushes, and now Barack Obama.

Obama, in enabling the Muslim Brotherhood and other Islamic *jihadist* entities, is following in the policy footsteps of FDR in propping up the Soviet Union, and of Ronald Reagan, whom we should thank for enabling the Taliban and Al-Qada, for once the Islamists had finished defeating the Soviets in Afghanistan, they turned their sights and guns on the West.

JFK, in his undelivered Dallas speech, whether he knew it or not, addressed the legacy of FDR's recognition of the Soviet government as a legitimate one and of how he conducted WWII as a virtual valet to Josef Stalin's wishes.

On the other hand, Obama has never much disguised in his banal rhetoric his hostility to freedom. His friendship with the Muslim Brotherhood and its operatives in and out of this country's government, and now coupled with his surrender to Iran in Geneva over Iran's nuclear program, compounds the error made by Reagan in aiding Islamic designs on the West, by further emulating FDR's pro-Soviet policies.

In this light, Neville Chamberlain was not the only appeaser of tyranny, and, as with Chamberlain, peace will not be had in our time.

Barack Obama is also "charting our destinies," in which death by ObamaCare or death by an Iranian-designed nuclear bomb detonated in Israel or the U.S. is the destination.

Obama is no appeaser of tyranny. All indications are that he is its friend and ally.

November 2013

James Madison vs. Frank Nitti

Daniel Greenfield, in his Sultan Knish column, "The Chicagozation of America" (April 11th), remarked about the workings of urban machine politics:

> In 2012, tribal politics became national politics. The country was divided and conquered. A campaign run on convincing a dozen separate groups to be afraid of each other and of the majority made all the difference, not in some urban slum, but from sea to shining sea. The country had at last become the city. And considering the state of the city... the state of the union does not look good.

His column featured a photograph of Saul Alinsky, author of *Rules for Radicals* and other *Democracy for Dummies and Democrats* tracts that serve as hands-on instruction manuals for liberals, leftists, and out-and-out communists and socialists in how to acquire power and disenfranchise everyone but their patrons. In other words, elective gangsters. Such as Barack Obama, and Hillary Clinton, who admired Alinsky and his "community organizing" philosophy so much she wrote her Wellesley senior thesis on them and even interviewed Alinsky.

Greenfield does not mention Alinsky in the column, which is about how "democracy" has become a game and tactic of criminal politicians who manipulate contentious voting blocs and vested interests. He did not need to. Alinsky's face and that photograph in particular are too familiar. Alinsky boasted that he befriended and fraternized with Chicago gangsters. That is entirely appropriate, given the state of Chicago and American politics as described by Greenfield.

Here is an anecdote in Alinsky's own words about how cozy he was with Frank Nitti, Al Capone's "enforcer." Nitti liked Alinsky and allowed him to look over the criminal's books:

> Once, when I was looking over their records, I noticed an item listing a $7500 payment for an out-of-town killer. I called Nitti over and I said, "Look, Mr. Nitti, I don't understand this. You've got at least 20 killers on your

payroll. Why waste that much money to bring somebody in from St. Louis?" Frank was really shocked at my ignorance.

"Look, kid," he said patiently, "sometimes our guys might know the guy they're hitting, they may have been to his house for dinner, taken his kids to the ball game, been the best man at his wedding, gotten drunk together. But you call in a guy from out of town, all you've got to do is tell him, 'Look, there's this guy in a dark coat on State and Randolph; our boy in the car will point him out; just go up and give him three in the belly and fade into the crowd.' So that's a job and he's a professional, he does it. But one of our boys goes up, the guy turns to face him and it's a friend, right away he knows that when he pulls that trigger there's gonna be a widow, kids without a father, funerals, weeping -- Christ, it'd be murder."

Such was the wisdom imbibed by Saul Alinsky, amoral and pragmatist tactician and organizer of other criminal mobs, otherwise known as the Left. For what is the Left but a loose alliance of ideological gangsters who rationalize and sanction force, but who pose as "humanitarians" sensitive to the feelings of others? Gangster government, indeed.

But, in this column we will not be "going there." I don't think it's necessary to compare Alinsky's foul character with that of James Madison. That would be an insult to Madison. This column will dwell on a species of wisdom not possible to Alinsky, Frank Nitti, or even to any contemporary politician. Here, in speeches, separate correspondence and in his Federalist Papers, are some excerpted thoughts and cogitations of Madison, one of our Founders, defending and explaining the workings of the federal Constitution after it had been framed in 1787 Philadelphia. The document had been sent out to all the states for debate and ratification. A multitude of objections to it, some valid, some specious, were cropping up and distracting everyone's attention. Madison felt obliged to defend the document and to refute all the criticisms of it that came his way. Originally, he questioned the wisdom of including a "bill of rights" that would specifically obstruct federal incursions on specific realms of individual liberty.

But in June of 1789, he submitted a bill of rights to a Congress embroiled in other issues. He became known as the "father" of the Bill of Rights – rights which Congress today is contemplating their suspension or nullification.

All quotations are from *James Madison: Writings**, and are followed by the referenced page numbers. Quotations have been edited for archaic spelling, punctuation and formatting. Notes in square brackets are my own interjections on meaning and context for clarity's sake.

In a letter to William Bradford in January 1774, before the Revolution began, Madison remarked:

> ...Political contests are necessary sometimes as well as military to afford exercise and practice and to instruct in the Art of defending Liberty and property....If the Church of England had been established and general Religion in all the Northern Colonies as it has been among us here and uninterrupted tranquility had prevailed throughout the Continent, it is clear to me that slavery and subjection [subjugation or submission] might and would have been gradually insinuated among us. (p. 5)

Here Madison was exhibiting prescience, not only about his later task of construing the Constitution for his readers, but was commenting on how a state religion can suppress liberty. He would later call for the separation of church and state. We now have two state "religions" that perform that role: environmentalism and "gay marriage," and the state has been empowered to enforce obeisance to both.

In a speech before the Convention in June, 1787, Madison inveighed against "pure" democracy, and warned how religion and combative blocs in a population would lead to anarchy and tyranny.

> In all cases where a majority are united by a common interest or passion, the rights of the minority are in danger....Religion itself may become a motive to persecution and oppression. These observations are verified by the Histories of every Country ancient and modern. In Greece and Rome, the rich and poor, the creditors and debtors, as

well as the patricians and plebians alternately oppressed each other with equal unmercifulness. (pp. 92-93)

In this same speech, Madison endorsed the idea of dividing the federal government into three branches – the executive, the legislative, and a senate – and prohibiting the branches from developing overlapping authorities. We don't see much of that separation today. The only branch that has retained some independence from the other branches is the Supreme Court, but that separation can be nullified by an executive or president who seeks to pack the Court with justices friendly to his agenda. Senate confirmation hearings on Court nominees are supposed to weed out those who are hostile or ambivalent to a strict reading of the Constitution. That has not happened.

On the role of the Senate, Madison had this to say at the Convention, in answer to another delegate's proposal to make the Senate as large as the House of Representatives:

> The use of the Senate is to consist in its proceeding with more coolness, with more system, and with more wisdom, than the popular branch. Enlarge their number and you communicate to them the vices which they are meant to correct. (p. 98)

The function of the Senate, to act as a check on populist legislation and causes with its "coolness and wisdom," was annulled by the Seventeenth Amendment in 1913 which allowed the direct or popular election of U.S. senators, instead of by state legislatures. Nineteen-thirteen was a banner year for Progressive statism. The Sixteenth Amendment or the Income Tax Amendment was ratified in February, and the Federal Reserve Act was enacted in December.

On July 20th, 1787, Madison addressed the Convention on the subject of executive powers and the impeachment of the president.

> Mr. Madison thought it indispensable that some provision should be made for defending the Community against the incapacity, negligence or perfidy of the chief Magistrate. The limitation of the period of his service was not sufficient security....He might pervert his administration into a scheme

of peculation or oppression. He might betray his trust to foreign powers. (p. 128)

This projection of the executive branch's potential depredations can be applied to any number of administrations since, say, President Grant's term, but it certainly describes that of Barack Obama. Anyone remember Solyndra, or Obama's assurances to dictator Vladimir Putin that, once he was reelected, he would have "more flexibility" in compromising this country's ability to defend itself?

But Madison could not imagine that the whole of Congress could become so corrupted as to pose just as perilous a danger to the country as would a president wielding dictatorial powers.

> The case of the Executive Magistracy was very distinguishable from that of the Legislature....It could not be presumed that all or even a majority of the members of an Assembly would either lose their capacity for discharging, or be bribed to betray their trust. Besides the restraints of their personal integrity and honor, the difficulty of acting in concert for purposes of corruption was a security to the public. And if one or a few members only should be seduced, the soundness of the remaining members would maintain the integrity and fidelity of the body....(p. 128)

Do we laugh now, or later? There are only a handful of Senators and Representatives who are "restrained" by their personal integrity and honor from feeding with the rest of Congress at the spend-and-tax-and-regulate trough. Madison can be forgiven for his naïveté. He lived in an era of intellectual giants, and presumed the swine of his time would be kept in their pigpens.

Madison forecast the problems with universal suffrage and recommended that the power to vote for any candidates in national and state elections be limited to property owners. In a speech to the Convention August 1787, he explained why:

> The right of suffrage is certainly one of the fundamental articles of republican Government. A gradual abridgment of this right has been the mode in which Aristocracies have

> been built on the ruins of popular forms....In several of the States a freehold was now the qualification. Viewing the subject in its merits alone, the freeholders of the Country would be the safest depositories of Republican liberty. In future times a great majority of the people will not only be without landed but without any other sort of property. These will either combine under the influence of their common situation, in which case the rights and public liberty will not be secure in their hands; or which is more probable, they will become the tools of opulence and ambition, in which case there will be equal danger on another side. (pp. 132-133)

In short, Madison was saying that those who owned land would be more likely to defend its sanctity *and* their individual rights than would a "democratic" mob that wished to expropriate it, and vote for individuals who were pledged to protect it against populist measures and clamors to "narrow the gap" between the rich and the poor. Madison could not have imagined a federal government that had the power to "narrow the gap" with powers not enumerated in the Constitution. Neither he nor even the most ardent Federalist, such as Alexander Hamilton (who also contributed to the Federalist), could have predicted the mammoth, wealth-consuming welfare state that cripples the economy and redirects (or "redistributes") the productive energies of the country to the omnivorous, bottomless pit of the unproductive and anti-productive.

Of course, today, if suffrage was to be based on property ownership, the definition of property would need to be expanded to include other kinds of property as well as land, such as private home ownership and one's estimated worth in the way of stock holdings and derived income. But, this is a technical issue beyond the ken of contemporary theorists and politicians.

In a long letter to Thomas Jefferson in October 1787, Madison remarked on the foolhardiness of democracy and the dangers it posed to an individual rights-protecting republic. Jefferson was in France during the Convention. It would be intriguing to speculate on the character of the Constitution had he attended the Convention.

> Those who contend for a simple Democracy, or a pure republic, actuated by the sense of the majority, and operating

within narrow limits, assume or suppose a case which is altogether fictitious....A distinction of property results from that very protection which a free Government gives to unequal faculties of acquiring it. There will be rich and poor, creditors and debtors, a landed interest, a monied interest, a mercantile [commercial or business] interest, a manufacturing interest....(p. 150)

But, Madison wrote, these different classes needn't be hostile to each other nor be in political conflict with each other as long as the government did not favor one over the other with special legislation, that is, for example, if neither Congress nor the executive branch were open to subornation by lobbyists and other special interests.

In the same letter to Jefferson, Madison listed three motives which he thought would *not* protect individuals or a minority against the actions of a democratic mob or act as guarantors of individual rights: "A prudent regard to private or partial good...Respect for character....Religion." Of religion, he said:

When indeed Religion is kindled into enthusiasm, its force like that of other passions is increased by the sympathy of a multitude. But enthusiasm is only a temporary state of Religion, and while it lasts will hardly been seen with pleasure at the helm. Even in its coolest state it has been much oftener a motive to oppression than a restraint from it....(p. 151)

In his Federalist No. 10, Madison noted the dangers and impracticality of democracies, big and small. In a "pure" democracy

A common passion or interest will, in almost every case, be felt by a majority of the whole; a communication and concert results from the form of government itself, and there is nothing to check the inducements to sacrifice the weaker party, or the obnoxious individual. Hence it is that such democracies have ever been spectacles of turbulence and contention, have ever been found incompatible with personal security, or the rights of property, and have in general been

> as short in their lives as they have been violent in their deaths....
>
> Men of factious tempers, of local prejudices, or of sinister designs, may intrigue by corruption or by other means, first obtain the suffrages, and then betray the interests of the people.... (pp. 164-165)

What a fitting description of how Barack Obama has won two presidential elections. He is, after all, a man of "factious temper" with an agenda of "sinister designs."

Finally, Madison had something to say about the differences between a democracy and a constitutional republic, and in Federalist No. 14 wrote in answer to critics of the Constitution who alleged that a constitutional republic was as dangerous as a pure democracy:

> ....A republic may be extended over a large region [i.e., continental North America]. To this accidental source of the error may be added the artifice of some celebrated authors whose writings have had a great share in forming the modern standard of political opinions. Being subjects either of an absolute or limited monarchy, they have endeavored to heighten the advantages or palliate the evils of those forms by placing in comparison with them the vices and defects of the republican, and by citing as specimens of the latter, the turbulent democracies of ancient Greece and modern Italy. Under the confusion of names, it has been an easy task to transfer to a republic observations applicable to a democracy only....(pp. 168-169)

It is a confusion which persists to this day, when even advocates of limited government, such as the Tea Party, persistently refer to our republic as a "democracy," unable or unwilling to distinguish between the two systems, thinking that no distinction exists or is necessary.

Madison penned twenty-six more Federalist numbers, the last in March 1788. But you cannot help but scream to the ceiling when comparing his grasp of political principles and folly with the unadulterated folly, ignorance, and indifference paraded by contemporary politicians and even theorists. Today's politicians are not Madison's intellectual heirs; they are Alinsky's, and Frank Nitti's, with numerous political go-betweens on the descent to legislative thuggery and imbecility: the prim and proper Progressive Woodrow Wilson; the disgraceful Warren G. Harding; the socialist opportunist Franklin D. Roosevelt; the pouting thug Harry S. Truman (the model for Ayn Rand's "chief of state" villain, Mr. Thompson, in *Atlas Shrugged*); the bland nonentity Dwight D. Eisenhower; the fascist John F. Kennedy. And all of those who followed, including Ronald Reagan.

The collectivist pot has boiled away, and what is left in it is the heir and essence of collectivism: Barack Hussein Obama, the mean, small, malevolent, arrogant graduate of the Alinsky-Nitti School of Practical Statism, who has succeeded in "Chicagoizing" the American Republic.

James Madison: Writings. New York: The Library of America, 1999. Ed. Jack N. Rakove.

April 2013

Justice Stevens's
Liberty-Destroying Amendments Part I

The liberal/left is forever releasing trial balloons to see who shoots at them and who doesn't. The multiple interviews of retired Supreme Court Justice John Paul Stevens upon publication of his new book, *Six Amendments: How and Why We Should Change the Constitution,* on April 22nd, represent one such balloon. I have not yet read the book, but have ordered it and will review it in a future column. But the lubricious reception of Stevens's book and the unrestrained fawning over him by the press is such that I can't hold my tongue. So these remarks will focus on the interviews, and not the book *per se*.

The book would not be reviewed, nor Stevens even interviewed, but for the liberty-destroying amendments he proposes be made to the Constitution. Liberal "journalists" across the spectrum sidled up to the buffet and feasted on helpings of the retired liberal, pro-government power justice's fare of senile lunacy, washed down with large draughts of Happy Juice.

All the interviewers treated Stevens as a kind of judicial "guru" whose "wisdom" must be shown deference and couldn't be challenged or questioned without committing a heinous *faux pas*. They asked him leading questions to prompt the answers they wanted to hear from Stevens. For example, in the video on the NRO site, George Stephanopoulos asks Stevens about the five words Stevens would add to the "amended" Second Amendment: "...the right of the people to keep and bear arms [*when serving in the militia*] shall not be infringed."

The "militia" meaning the National Guard or virtually any federal SWAT or armed enforcement entity. It means that the government would have a monopoly on all weapons.

> Stephanopoulos: "Wouldn't that take away any limits what a legislature could do to the rights of gun owners?"
>
> Stevens: "I think that's probably right." [Still of rows of hand guns] "I think that's what should be the rule, that it should be legislatures rather than judges who draw the line on what is permissible...."

Stephanopoulos: "Do you think that....clearly...that was what was intended?"

Stevens: "I do think that was what was originally intended, because there was a fear among the original framers that the federal government would be so strong that they might destroy the state militias. The amendment would merely *prevent arguments being made that Congress doesn't have the power to do what is in the best public interest.*" [More "scary" images of weapons; *Italics* mine]

Stephanopoulos: "But to be clear, if Congress passed a national ban on individual gun ownership, that would be constitutional under your amendment?"

Stevens: "I think that's right."

Have an argument that questions Congress's power to enforce gun-control? Stow it. Stevens's amendment forbids you to make it. Are you against the "public interest," or what, you unpatriotic American!

Stevens's amendment makes no sense at all. The right to bear arms *as a private citizen* either is or isn't "infringed." If it *is* infringed upon, then the only time you can exercise your "right" is when you're working for the government enforcing the government's will at gunpoint (lawfully or unlawfully). Then, when the task is completed, you would hand the weapon you used back to the armorer. You may "bear" the arms, but not own it.

If it *isn't* infringed upon, then you may own and "bear arms," certainly without leave of the authorities, and without having to serve in any government policing or military force. Period.

And Stevens's secret, unspoken thought at that point: *Thank you, Mr. Stephanopoulos, for putting those words in my mouth. I couldn't have said it better myself.* What an instance of evasion by Stevens! What an example of prompting by Stephanopoulos! But this is his usual interrogative habit: acting like a theatrical prompter cueing Stevens on the right lines.

In the Framers' time, state militias were drawn from a population of armed citizens. Stevens can't have been ignorant of this fact. What the Framers had in mind when including that amendment was not only the ability of states to protect their sovereignty from federal power, but also the ability of private citizens to protect themselves from federal power, as well. The Framers were thinking in fundamentals.

Of course, long ago the states surrendered their sovereignty by becoming addicted – sometimes at extortionate gunpoint, but too often not – to federal largesse various forms drawn from a national taxpayer population. States have become submissive and dependent satrapies of the central federal government.

Richard Wolf, in his April 21st USA TODAY article, "Former justice Stevens wants to change the Constitution," opens with:

> Former Supreme Court justice John Paul Stevens wants to reduce gun violence, abolish the death penalty, restrict political campaign spending, limit states' independence and make Congress more competitive and less combative. His solution: Amend the Constitution....

> "It's certainly not easy to get the Constitution amended, and perhaps that's one flaw in the Constitution that I don't mention in the book," he said during a wide-ranging interview with USA TODAY in his chambers at the court. Noting his book's half dozen proposed amendments, he mused, "Maybe I should have had seven."

A seventh amendment to allow easier gutting of the Constitution? Why not? What Stevens proposes would be a step in the right direction. I mean, the *left* direction.

> Though Stevens proposes precise language for each proposed amendment, he admits the process is extremely difficult. It takes two-thirds of both houses of Congress or state legislatures to propose an amendment and three-fourths of the legislatures to approve it. The last amendment, blocking Congress from changing its members' salaries between elections, passed in 1992.

Wolf reports:

> Among the amendments Stevens suggests:
>
> •Changing the Second Amendment to make clear that only a state's militia, not its citizens, has a constitutional right to bear arms.
>
> •Changing the Eighth Amendment's prohibition against "cruel and unusual punishments" by specifically including the death penalty.
>
> •Removing from First Amendment protection any "reasonable limits" on campaign spending enacted by Congress or the states.
>
> •Requiring that congressional and state legislative districts be "compact and composed of contiguous territory" to stop both parties from carving out safe seats.
>
> •Eliminating states' sovereign immunity from liability for violating the Constitution or an act of Congress, which he calls a "manifest injustice."
>
> •Allowing Congress to require states to perform federal duties in emergencies, in order to reduce "the risk of a national catastrophe."

What prompted Stevens to write *Six Amendments*?

> It was the December 2012 school shootings in Newtown, Conn., that focused Stevens' [*sic*] attention on a rule that prevents Congress from requiring states to perform federal duties. The rule had led to holes in a federal database of gun purchases.
>
> "It's called the anti-commandeering rule, which turned out to be the first chapter of a book that kind of grew like Topsy," Stevens said. "I thought that maybe the only way to get rid of the rule is to have a constitutional amendment, and then it

occurred to me ... that there really are other provisions of the Constitution that should be looked at more closely."

Wolf concludes his article with a friendly warning:

> Among the issues to watch for, [Stevens] said, are a constitutional right to same-sex marriage ("Sooner or later, they'll have to address the question"), gun control (Scalia's 2008 opinion protecting handguns in the home won't be the final word), and government surveillance programs, *which Stevens defends as constitutional*. [*Italics* mine]

As long as the government doesn't watch Muslims. In Stevens's mind, *anything* may be made constitutional – as long as it has nothing to do with individual rights, the sanctity of property, and an individual owning his own life, and not the state.

PBS Newhour's Judy Woodruff practically sat at Stevens's feet during her interview of Stevens, in "How retired Supreme Court Justice Stevens would amend the constitution," and prompted Stevens as well as Stephanopoulos had. On campaign finance:

> **JUDY WOODRUFF:** Another controversy you're jumping right into is campaign finance. You believe Congress should be able to put limits on the amount of money candidates spend on their campaigns...
>
> **FMR. JUSTICE JOHN PAUL STEVENS:** Yes.
>
> **JUDY WOODRUFF:** ... and that the Supreme Court has made mistakes in several decisions, allowing corporations, labor unions to advocate and spend money on candidates. Considering all the court has done, Justice Stevens, to open the door for huge money to pour into American politics, including the recent McCutcheon decision, what effect does all this have on American politics?

Judy Woodruff counts to three, and says quietly, "You're on!" Stevens answers:

FMR. JUSTICE JOHN PAUL STEVENS: Well, I don't think it's a healthy effect. And I think it's a change from what the people who direct — framed our basic government envisioned. For the — as the chief justice said, I think, in the first sentence of his opinion in the McCutcheon case the other day, there is nothing more important than participation in electing our representatives.

But the law that developed in that case and in a number of other cases involved not electing the representatives of the people who voted for them, but electing representatives of — in other jurisdictions where the financing is used. In other words, that was a case that involved the right of the — of an individual to spend as much of its money as he wanted to elect representatives of other people. He didn't use any of that money to elect his own representatives.

Meaning that one would not be allowed to donate money to the candidate or advocate of one's choice, except in amounts predetermined by the government or the Federal Election Commission. However, as an outraged Fred Wertheimer notes in his SCOTUS Blog:

With its *Citizens United* and *McCutcheon* decisions, the Supreme Court has turned our representative system of government into a sandbox for America's billionaires and millionaires to play in.

The Court's decisions have empowered a new class of American political oligarchs and have come at the enormous expense of the voices and interests of more than 300 million Americans.

Cloaked in jurisprudence, the five Justices who make up a majority on the Supreme Court are imposing their ideology and politics on the country. In the process, they are issuing radical, not conservative, opinions.

Meaning that opinions at odds with the reigning leftist ideology are to be feared; left-wing billionaires would be free to dominate the "sandbox" with impunity, as Barack Obama's donors and backers did in 2008 and 2012. That would be all right with Wertheimer – and Justice Stevens.

Woodruff turns to gun control and flashes Stevens her cue cards:

> **JUDY WOODRUFF:** The last area that I want to ask you about is what this country should do about guns. You would change the wording of the Second Amendment to the Constitution to say the right of people to bear arms to own a gun should apply only when serving in the militia. Is it your ultimate hope that there would be no right to own a gun for self-defense?

> **FMR. JUSTICE JOHN PAUL STEVENS:** Well, it would be my ultimate hope that legislatures would decide the issues, and not be hampered by constitutional restrictions, because, clearly, legislators are in a much better position than judges are to decide what could be permissible in different contexts.

> And the effect of the Second Amendment as it is now construed is to make federal judges the final arbiters of gun policy, which is quite, quite wrong, I think, and quite contrary to what the framers intended when they drafted the Second Amendment, to protect states from the danger that a strong federal armed force would have been able [*sic*] to the states of their own militias.

Finally, an April 21st, article in the New York Times, by Adam Liptak, who also interviewed, Stevens, "Justice Stevens Suggests Solution for 'Giant Step in the Wrong Direction," focuses on the campaign finance law.

> The occasion for our talk was Justice Stevens's new book, "Six Amendments: How and Why We Should Change the Constitution." One of those amendments would address Citizens United, which he wrote was "a giant step in the wrong direction."....

> He talked about what he called a telling flaw in the opening sentence of last month's big campaign finance ruling. He filled in some new details about the behind-the-scenes maneuvering that led to the Citizens United decision. And he called for a constitutional amendment to address what he

said was the grave threat to American democracy caused by the torrent of money in politics.

Last month's decision in McCutcheon v. Federal Election Commission struck down aggregate contribution limits, allowing rich people to make donations to an unlimited number of federal candidates.

Chief Justice John G. Roberts Jr. started his controlling opinion with a characteristically crisp and stirring opening sentence: "There is no right more basic in our democracy than the right to participate in electing our political leaders."

But that was misleading, Justice Stevens said. "The first sentence here," he said, "is not really about what the case is about."

Then what was it about, if not the right of citizens to participle in elections, regardless of their tax brackets? Well, it was about something else, about *not* allowing rich donors dominate and elections. Rich donors, of course, meaning rich "conservatives" like the Koch Brothers supporting candidates who oppose big government. Rich donors and manipulators like George Soros should be exempt from campaign contribution laws and the number of candidates they can support in political action committees (PACs), under the table, and across state lines.

Liptak writes:

> The new amendment would override the First Amendment and allow Congress and the states to impose "reasonable limits on the amount of money that candidates for public office, or their supporters, may spend in election campaigns."

> I asked whether the amendment would allow the government to prohibit newspapers from spending money to publish editorials endorsing candidates. He stared at the text of his proposed amendment for a little while. "The 'reasonable' would apply there," he said, "or might well be construed to apply there."

> Or perhaps not. His tentative answer called to mind an exchange at the first Citizens United argument, when a government lawyer told the court that Congress could in theory ban books urging the election of political candidates. Justice Stevens said he would not go that far. "Perhaps you could put a limit on the times of publication or something," he said. "You certainly couldn't totally prohibit writing a book."

Well, why not? I'm sure a justice with Stevens's intellectual acumen could knock together an argument for prohibiting the publication of books critical of candidates and their agendas during an election cycle. That, of course, would be censorship.

The New York Times would howl like a stuck pig were it prohibited from editorializing about its favorite candidates. Political non-profits, and competing newspapers of the "conservative" bent, however, must gag themselves in a censorial "fairness doctrine," or else feel the weight of the FEC and the IRS.

Not to worry. Stevens is a little foggy on how he'd construe "reasonable." Note: The occasion of the publication of Stevens's book is about as trial balloon as you can get. After all, Stevens, now 94, still had enough energy to fit in numerous interviews with sympathetic, bedazzled journalists in the space of two days, doubtless with the cooperation of his publisher.

In the near future, I will take out my bow and arrow, and, emulating Katniss Everdeen (a mnemonic device for "Can't Miss Ever, Dear"?) of *The Hunger Games* movies, and puncture of few of the trial balloons in Stevens's book.

Six Amendments: How and Why We Should Change the Constitution, by John Paul Stevens. New York: Little, Brown and Company/Hachette Book Group, 2014. 192 pp.

May 2014

Justice Stevens's
Liberty-Destroying Amendments: Part II

As promised in Part I of this review of the reception by the press and news media of Justice John Paul's new book, *Six Amendments: How and Why We Should Change the Constitution*, I have read his book and now can review it here.

There is a prologue, an appendix containing the Constitution, and six chapters, each chapter devoted to one of Stevens's recommended amendments. At the end of each chapter, after lengthy and often in-depth discussions of the history and role of the existing amendment in Supreme Court and other federal court decisions, Stevens states his amendment. Stevens is an excellent writer. His prose is clear and unburdened by jargon and legalese. One supposes that is a natural consequence of having written numerous 100-page or more opinions during a six-year stint on the U.S. 7th Circuit Court of Appeals, and then over a 35-year career on the Supreme Court.

Readers accustomed to encountering a concluding, assertive statement, followed by an explanation for the conclusion (e.g., at the beginning of a trial, a prosecutor would say, "The State will prove that John Doe murdered Bob Smith."), will experience a reversal of that usual order of reasoning, which employs deduction and often induction. Stevens instead explains first, and concludes with his opinion at the end of each chapter (e.g., "Here is what happened, and why, this is what X said and this is what Y said, and the timetable; and the jury, in the end, must find John Doe guilty of murder.").

Stevens's writing style, however, is double-edged, for his hostility towards the existing amendments to the Constitution, three of which he wishes to rewrite, and three new ones he wishes to be added, is made clearer. That hostility is not disguised by verbose and affected discourse or by a sophist's bewildering labyrinth of irrelevancies and false turns that would flat-line the mind of the sharpest reader. The six areas Stevens discusses are the "anti-commandeering" rule, political gerrymandering, campaign finance, sovereign immunity, the death penalty, and the Second Amendment (gun control). I shall address these subjects in the order in which Stevens presents them.

It would be fair to say up front that, in all cases and all issues he discusses, Stevens champions federal power and authority over that of the individual states (and, indirectly, over individual rights). In his Prologue, after briefly discussing how the withdrawal of federal troops in the Southern states in 1877 engendered the rise of the Ku Klux Klan (with the approbation of Southern Democrats), he inadvertently demonstrates how destructive Constitutional amendments can be.

> In 1913 two amendments to the Constitution were adopted. The Sixteenth Amendment overruled the five-to-four decision of the Supreme Court in *Pollock v. Farmers Loan and Trust Co.* which had held that a federal statute imposing a tax on income violated the constitutional prohibition against unapportioned "direct taxes"; that amendment is the source of the federal power to impose an income tax. The Seventeenth Amendment replaced the practice of having United States senators chosen by state legislatures with direct elections by the people.
>
> The Eighteenth Amendment, prohibiting the manufacture, sale, or transportation of intoxicating liquors, became effective in 1919; it was repealed by Section 1 of the Twenty-first Amendment in 1933. (pp. 9-10)

The destruction wrought by the Sixteenth Amendment needs no explication here. The Seventeenth Amendment clearly flies in the face of the Framers' intention to create a legislative body that would serve as a check on populist legislation emanating from the House, and which, as a body, would be imbued with a higher degree of wisdom and integrity in the name of individual rights and limited government. Today, the Senate is a mere echo chamber of the House's collectivist, statist agendas.

Reading *Pollok* case, it was interesting to learn that Congress had passed in income tax in 1894; the Supreme Court voided it in this case. It was also startling to learn that income taxes had been discussed in the early days of the Republic by some of the Framers. Abraham Lincoln signed the first income tax into law in 1861, to help finance the Civil War (it was repealed by Congress in 1872). And in every instance I could find, the issue confronting the opponents and advocates of income taxation of any kind was not the sanctity of private property, but rather the irrelevancies of whether or not the tax was a "direct" or "excise" tax, or whether or not it violated states' rights vis-à-vis apportionment, and other technicalities About *Pollock*, The Chicago-Kent College of Law site notes:

> The Court held that the act violated the Constitution [Article I, Section 9] since it imposed taxes on personal income derived from real estate investments and personal property such as stocks and bonds; this was a direct taxation scheme, not apportioned properly among the states. The decision was negated by the adoption of the Sixteenth Amendment in 1913.

In all of Stevens's proposals, the issue of individual rights is never brought to the fore, positively or negatively; it is though they did not exist for him. Individual rights are invisible, they do not exist in his universe of political propriety. It was only the powers of the State that must be elucidated and sorted out; those powers, to the retired Justice, are of paramount importance.

In Chapter 1, Stevens discusses the background of the so-called "anti-commandeering" rule, established in 1997 by the Supreme Court in *Printz v. United States*, "a rule that prohibits Congress from requiring state officials to perform federal duties," that is, "commandeering" the authority and persons of state or local officials to enforce federal law. *Printz* arose out of the attempted assassination of President Ronald Reagan in 1991, from the Gun Control Act of 1968 – "a detailed federal scheme governing the distribution of firearms" – and finally from the Brady Handgun Violence Act of 1993. Two law enforcement officers, one from Montana and one from Arizona, brought suit against the Brady Act that would establish a national background check system for buyers of firearms. They argued that it was an unconstitutional imposition on them to perform background checks at the behest of the federal government.

Stevens also, in the same chapter, includes the "commandeering" of state judges to enforce federal statutes. He regards it as disgraceful that state officials and state judges should be exempted from taking orders from the federal government to enforce its law. Why? Because it smacks of inefficiency when the federal government is pursuing a "common good" or acting in the "public interest."

> In addition to increasing the risk of a national catastrophe and hampering the federal government's ability to make a

prompt and effective response to disasters, the anti-commandeering rule also limits the government's options in the routine administration of its programs. Federal programs involving the protection of the environment, the distribution of electric power, and the regulation of interstate transportation, as examples, may be implemented more efficiently by the reliance, in part, on state personnel instead of enlarging the federal bureaucracy. (pp. 27-28)

It does not occur to Stevens that a supremely "efficient" government is a totalitarian one, one to be feared. An "inefficient" one is merely authoritarian or statist, sustained by a mixed economy of regulations, controls, and "conditional" freedoms of trade and speech. The Nazis and Soviets ran very "efficient" governments. Further, the existence of the "anti-commandeering" rule has not contributed to federal regulatory bureaucracies swelling in size and power. They do that because of their intrinsic nature, coupled with a vested interest in their growth by their champions in Congress, their directors or heads, and federal employee unions. Stevens concludes:

Adding just four words – "and other public officials" – immediately after the word "Judges" in the Supremacy Clause, would, under the Court's reasoning, expressly confirm the power of Congress to impose mandatory duties on public officials in every state. (p. 29)

I had expected Chapter 2, "Political Gerrymandering," to be dull, plodding reading, and, indeed it was. Stevens begins the chapter with an explanation of the term "gerrymander."

In 1811…the governor, Elbridge Gerry [of Massachusetts], and a majority of both branches of the legislature were Republican. In order to retain control of the government…they redrew the boundaries of the thirty senatorial districts, packing enough Federalists into a small number of districts to give the Republicans comfortable majorities in the others….The shapes of the districts drawn by Gerry's partisans were anything but compact. Because one of them resembled a salamander, contemporary newsmen coined the term "gerrymander" to describe the governor's electoral stratagem. Both the term and the stratagem have survived for the past two centuries. (pp. 33-34)

I will spare the reader Stevens's account of how gerrymandering was and is still practiced in the United States. It's much like describing how rival college fraternities and sororities conduct membership drives or "rushes" and divvy up campus turf in "spheres of influence." The issue, for Stevens, is one of fair or equal representation of an electorate that is at the mercy of the district line drawers. Stevens doesn't think they should have the power to disenfranchise one portion of the electorate at the expense of another. He writes:

> Admittedly, the Constitution does not require proportional representation, but there is a world of difference between such a strict requirement and a more limited prohibition against a political party's use of government power to draft bizarre districts that have no purpose or justification other than enhancing that party's own power. Just as a controlling political party may not use public funds to pay its campaign expenses, it is also quite wrong to use public power for the sole purpose of enhancing the political strength of the majority party. (pp. 47-48)

That was just an introduction to Stevens's real concern:

> As discussed above, the gerrymandering process makes elections – both in districts the majority expects to carry, and in districts packed with voters who belong to the minority party – less competitive, and leads candidates, whether liberal or conservative, to adopt more extreme positions. *Ending political gerrymandering will help promote political compromise.* (pp. 53-54; *Italics* mine)

To end the nasty phenomenon of "extremism" and to foster the habit of compromise, Stevens recommends the following fresh new amendment to the Constitution;

> Districts represented by members of Congress, or by members of any state legislative body, shall be compact and composed of contiguous territory. The state shall have the burden of justifying any departures from this requirement by

> reference to neutral criteria such as natural, political, or historic boundaries or demographic changes. The interest in enhancing or preserving the political party in control of the state government is not such a neutral criterion. (p. 55)

And what unbiased politico or consultant would establish that "neutral criteria"? Would a Federal Election Commission-like bureaucracy enforce it? And, it seems that any party that advocates individual rights (e.g., the Tea Party) must compromise with statists and Progressives in the holy spirit of "compromise." Regardless of whether or not gerrymandering has governed the outcome of elections, that is precisely what has been happening without Stevens's new amendment.

On to Chapter 3, "Campaign Finance." Ever since the Supreme Court's *Citizens United v. Federal Election Commission* ruling in 2010, liberals and Progressives like Stevens have been in a dither, if not in a rabid state of outrage. Corporations and businesses are as invisible to Stevens as individual rights, and have no First Amendment, freedom of speech protections. However, Oyez distills the muddled premises and reasoning of the ruling, for it was not an overwhelming victory for Citizens United.

> The majority maintained that political speech is indispensable to a democracy, which is no less true because the speech comes from a corporation. The majority also held that the BCRA's disclosure requirements [Bipartisan Campaign Reform Act (BCRA) of 2002, which established the Federal Election Commission or FEC] as applied to *The Movie* were constitutional, reasoning that disclosure is justified by a "governmental interest" in providing the "electorate with information" about election-related spending resources. The Court also upheld the disclosure requirements for political advertising sponsors and it upheld the ban on direct contributions to candidates from corporations and unions.

At issue was a movie released by Citizens United, *Hillary: The Movie*, which portrayed Hillary Clinton as unqualified to be president. Citizens United, a well-endowed political action committee (PAC), wanted to televise the movie within the FEC-enforced 30-day "gagging" period during a local or national election, in this instance, during the 2008 presidential primaries. The FEC had determined that neither the movie nor

Citizens United was protected by the First Amendment, because, at any rate, Citizens United was a corporation, and that the movie itself was "campaign speech" that was restricted during a national election cycle. Citizens United sued the FEC over the various restrictions placed on corporations, citing violations of the First Amendment.

Stevens writes that there is nothing to fear from his proposed amendment:

> A constitutional amendment authorizing Congress and the states to place "reasonable" limitations on campaign expenditures would allow corporations to make public announcements of their views but would prohibit them from engaging in the kind of repetitive and excessive advocacy that the candidates typically employ. It would also repudiate both the holding and the reasoning in the *Citizens United* case, giving corporations an unlimited right to spend their shareholders' money in election campaigns. (p. 78)

Do the shareholders want a corporation to spend their money advocating issues? To Stevens, their wishes are irrelevant. Do individuals who encounter "repetitive and excessive" advocacy mind such encounters? That's irrelevant, too. Of course, those on the opposite side of an issue might mind it, but, like Muslims who object to critical things being said and written about Islam, they can just ignore it. Speech, written, oral, or visually, after all, is not a form of physical aggression or force. But Stevens doesn't want the champions of big government and incremental socialism to be subjected to such "hate speech" over and over again. Poor babies! Stevens's suggested amendment, which does require force, reads:

> Neither the First Amendment nor any other provision of this Constitution shall be construed to prohibit the Congress or any state from imposing reasonable limits on the amount of money that candidates for public office, or their supporters, may spend in election campaigns. (p. 79)

Who will define what is "reasonable" and what is not? Is there an infallible mathematical formula that would define "reasonableness"? It would be okay, by Stevens, to abridge the scope of the First Amendment and thus violate its essential, fundamental meaning, just a little bit, to shut those wealthy, anti-big-government people up, and a public service, as well, don't you see?

A telling aspect of Stevens's book is that nowhere in his discussion of campaign finance does he address the influence of liberal/Progressive billionaires and millionaires on the political process, nor their own humongous contributions to the Democrats and liberal programs, nor the overflowing war chests and coffers of the Democratic Party in any given year. But, like the IRS, when it targeted conservative or Tea Party groups for audits and special scrutiny, but largely ignored the "deprecations" of liberal groups, the Federal Election Commission has a record of ignoring liberal/Progressive groups and fishing for evidence of wrongdoing by conservative or anti-big-government groups.

I don't think senility can explain that particular omission in Justice Stevens's book.

Part III of this column will discuss the last three of his proposed amendments, "Sovereignty," the death penalty, and the Second Amendment.

May 2014

Justice Stevens's
Liberty-Destroying Amendments: Part III

I ended Part II of this review by remarking on Retired Supreme Court Justice John Paul Stevens's treatment of the campaign finance law, the First Amendment, and freedom of speech in his book, *Six Amendments: How and Why We Should Change the Constitution*. Then this dropped into my in basket: Donald Sterling's "racist" rant in an illegally recorded private conversation that was released to the public. I had to address the subject, otherwise the issue would sit as a gnawing distraction in my craw.

I am not a fan or follower of any sport. For a while, I wondered what all the fuss was about concerning L.A. Clippers owner Donald Sterling. Spiked, a British news and column blog, ran an excellent article by Sean Collins on how private remarks about race or religion can lead to charges of bigotry or "hate speech" by the press and news media, and also by private citizens. The danger to freedom of speech, Collins writes in his April 30th article, "Not So Sterling Attack on Free Speech," is that,

> Those who warn about the NSA spying on every conversation are now among the loudest cheering Sterling's downfall, which wouldn't have happened without illegally obtained evidence. Do we really want to make pillow talk fair game? Expect more 'gotcha' stories, with leading figures being 'outed' for private comments recorded surreptitiously....
>
> Sterling's downfall came from impolitic speech, not from causing any actual harm....
>
> Many will say that this is not a free-speech issue, because Sterling did not have his First Amendment rights taken away, and the government did not step in to censor him. But free speech is more than legal rights *vis à vis* the state; it also includes whether we tolerate expression in society. Much of the debate over Sterling, as in other recent controversies (like the ousting of Brendan Eich at Mozilla), focuses on how the owners, boards of directors or managers should or shouldn't respond. But the real issue is not how those few at the top respond; it's how people in society respond.

And the problem today is that the broader response is intolerant: say something we deem unacceptable, and you must disappear. It would be perfectly fine – indeed a good thing, in my view – to express disagreement and disgust with racist views, and to argue against them in the strongest terms. But that's not the response we see today. Instead, it is 'make it go away now'. It's really problematic when people feel that the only way to express anger or opposition to something objectionable is to call for the one voicing that opinion to be hounded out.

I think even Collins misinterprets Sterling's remarks. However, he concludes his article with a warning:

Today, too many people are so convinced that they are in the right, that they are fighting bigotry and hatred, that they fail to see how their response is truly intolerant and illiberal. It's becoming almost automatic that, whenever something politically incorrect is uttered, a mob with pitchforks and torches rises up, seeking revenge and punishment. That response is unthinking, emotional and blind to the long-term consequences for a free society.

So, I listened to the TMZ tape, twice in case I missed something, the first time bracing myself to hear an incoherent, expletive-rich tirade by Sterling on blacks and Hispanics. Instead, I was surprised to learn that Sterling made *no* racist remarks at all, and that if an accusation of "racism" is to be leveled on anyone, it should be laid on V. Stiviano, his former girlfriend, with whom he was having a contentious conversation about her obsession with her "mixed" white and Mexican ancestry and showing off with black sports figures. I was so startled by what Sterling *did not* say, and what V. Stiviano *did say*, I left this comment on Collins's article:

Listening to the TMZ tape, I failed to detect any "racism" in Sterling's remarks. In fact, I'd say the "racism" is all on the woman's side. His complaint -- which he didn't or couldn't articulate -- is that she has no sense of privacy and feels compelled to flaunt her skin color or whatever publicly. He doesn't understand why she does that. Also, now that I've listened to the tape twice, I suspect that she [V. Stiviano] had

101.

the whole conversation recorded for some vendetta reason, and that she's responsible for its publication. All I hear in the tape are the protestations of a man being hounded by a "race conscious" bimbo, whose only claim to fame is that she was once Sterling's girlfriend. But, leave it to the "race conscious" news media to quote him out of context.

I think I know Cliven Bundy, who was also unjustifiably accused of racism, better than I ever would want to know Donald Sterling, but I can commiserate with Sterling, as well, up to a point (he has a reputation for uttering racist remarks and behaving badly to "minorities"). Both men are not the most well-spoken and articulate individuals by any means. They were average individuals addressing a difficult subject, Sterling in a verbal clinch with a whiney, half-*Chicana*, publicity-seeking harpy.

Sterling's "racist" remarks on the tape are so elusive, ambiguous, and open to interpretation, one can't even cherry-pick his responses to Stiviano's nagging and conclude that he was a dyed-in-the-wool racist (if you knew nothing else about him, which I didn't). One could conclude that he was lacking in character and independent judgment, yes. But racism? Hardly. Not in Stiviano's tape.

Now that I've dealt with the brainless sock puppets of the news media, I urge readers to listen to the TMZ tape and judge for themselves. Stiviano has since been interviewed by Barbara Walters on "20/20" and is singing another song.

That being said, let's tackle Justice Stevens's ideas on sovereign immunity in Chapter 4 of his book.

The subject is whether or not a state can be taken to court by residents or citizens of another state, or is immune or indemnified from such suits, or is not immune because it is not in compliance with federal law. The chapter also deals with whether or not the federal government can be sued by individuals. The Tenth, Eleventh and Fourteenth Amendments of the Constitution played a role in past Supreme Court decisions. Stevens provides a history of the issue and concludes that states and state officers should have no protection or defense if they are in violation of federal law. The Supreme Court has always been split on whether or not states are protected by the Eleventh Amendment:

> "The Judicial power of the United States shall not be construed to extend to any suit in law or equity, commenced or prosecuted against one of the United States by Citizens of another State, or by Citizens or Subjects of any Foreign State."

While the history of this issue is as muddled and governed by non-essentials as other issues discussed by Stevens, governed as it is by attention to procedural niceties and a hypothetical deference to federal authority (and Stevens's predecessors on the Court were as guilty of that as he is), I found the whole subject irrelevant, because all the states today are fiscally beholden to the federal government via a cornucopia of "entitlements" and bribes in terms of subsidies, grants and various welfare programs. To begin with, the states surrendered their "sovereignty" the moment they agreed to accept federal money for anything, whether to build highways or adopt federal standards of education in public schools.

Criticizing the Court's latest decision that perpetuated the notion of sovereign immunity, Stevens writes:

> Congress's power to enact laws that impose obligations on states and state agencies should include the power to authorize effective remedies for violations of those federal commands. (p. 105)

But, which commands? Which laws? Stevens makes no distinction between legitimate, proper laws, and fiat laws that "regulate" or abridge individual rights. As noted in Part II, Stevens does not even seem to be conscious of individual rights. They never enter into his calculations about what to do about alleged inequities in constitutional law.

His new amendment to the Constitution would read:

> Neither the Tenth Amendment, the Eleventh Amendment, nor any other provision of this Constitution, shall be construed to provide any state, state agency, or state officer with an immunity from liability for violating any act of Congress, or any provision of this Constitution. (p. 106)

In Chapter 5, "The Death Penalty," Stevens tackles capital punishment. Early on, he rejects, or at least questions, the usual arguments in favor of the death penalty: as a deterrent to crime, especially murder; and as retribution. Of the two, Stevens thinks the second justification is more plausible than the first.

> It can no longer be argued that execution of a potentially dangerous offender is necessary in order to remove the risk that he will commit further crimes. And the notion that the possible imposition of a death sentence is a significant deterrent on potential murderers must be modified to evaluate the marginal difference between the deterrent effect of that possible sentence and the deterrent effect of a sentence of life imprisonment without the possibility of parole. It is unlikely that criminals contemplating vicious crimes engage in the kind of cost-benefit analysis that would draw a distinction between those sentences. The real justification for preserving capital punishment surely rests on the interest of retribution. (pp. 109-110)

For once, I agree in part with Stevens. If one examines how some of the most vicious crimes have been committed, they do not seem to have been committed by perpetrators worried about the possible consequences in a court of law. They were committed by the perpetrators under the delusional hubris that they could get away with it, while they were on a "psychological high of invincibility." More often than not, they bungle the crime and leave evidence of their culpability behind; that is, it is only *after* the commission of the crime that they begin to be concerned about the possible consequences, and take precautionary actions to cover it up or leave evidence intended to mislead investigators away from their culpability and responsibility.

Stevens writes:

> ...I am convinced that the question whether we should retain the death penalty depends on the strength of the interest in retribution – the interest in avenging the harms caused by the most vicious criminals. (p. 110)

Retribution and justice, however, are not necessarily synonymous. In countries or societies governed by the rule of law, vengeance can be visited on murderers only as an afterthought, as an attendant, secondary consequence after a concern for justice. But, so much human history is a bloody record of retribution and vengeance, when the real or alleged crimes of a few are blamed on whole populations or groups and those populations or groups are made to pay the price for others' actions. The Hatfields and the McCoys, the Holocaust, the interminable tribal warfare among Muslims, are examples of *collectivist* notions of retribution and vengeance, and often excused by the perpetrators of the massacres, genocides, and pogroms as "justice."

Stevens references two cases, both of which required some form of capital punishment, *Florida v. Nixon* (2004) and *Baze v. Rees* (2008) to illustrate commonly held notions of retribution and the Eighth Amendment prohibition against "cruel and unusual punishment) and why he thinks they miss the mark in their intentions.

The first case concerned Joe Elton Nixon, who murdered a young woman by tying her to a tree with jumper cables and set her on fire with her belongings. Stevens notes that her "charred body made it obvious she had suffered a gruesome, excruciatingly painful death." (See Daniel Greenfield's article about a similar crime and the controversy over the botched execution of another convicted murderer.)

Nixon had already been convicted and sentenced to death by Florida. Nixon appealed claiming that he had not been consulted by his attorney on a plea of guilty. The Chicago-Kent College of Law noted:

> After several appeals the Florida Supreme Court granted Nixon a new trial. The court said Nixon's lawyer's comments were essentially a guilty plea and that because Nixon did not explicitly agree to the strategy, the lawyer was "per se ineffective."

However, an appeal to the highest court in the nation found that:

> In a unanimous 8-0 decision, the Court ruled that Nixon's lawyer's strategy - pursued without Nixon's express approval - did not automatically qualify the lawyer as ineffective. The Court reversed the ruling of the Florida Supreme Court, faulting that court for inappropriately applying presumptions of prejudice and deficient performance.

The second case involved a suit brought against the state of Kentucky by two convicts who claimed that certain drugs used by the state during executions were ineffective in preventing pain in the subject. The Chicago-Kent College of Law noted:

> In a 7-2 decision with four concurrences and a dissent, the Court held that Kentucky's lethal injection scheme did not violate the Eighth Amendment. Noting that the inmates had conceded the "humane nature" of the procedure when performed correctly, the divided Court [concluded that the] inmates had failed to prove that incorrect administration of the drugs would amount to cruel and unusual punishment....Justice John Paul Stevens wrote a separate concurring opinion supporting the judgment but for the first time stated his opposition to the death penalty.

Reviewing the opinions that concurred in both cases, vis-à-vis the notion of retribution and causing (or avoiding) pain in the executed, Stevens wrote:

> ...But even under his view [Justice Clarence Thomas's] the interest in retribution would not justify any attempt to apply an "eye for an eye" standard of punishment. Just as the *Nixon* case and its aftermath illustrate the waning public support for using the death penalty to avenge serious crimes, the *Baze* case reminds us that the Court has already developed a rule of law that prohibits states from subjecting the defendant to the kind of pain that he inflicted on his victim. (pp. 118-119)

Following that summation, Stevens then wrote:

> The requirement that guilt of a criminal charge be established by proof beyond a reasonable doubt has been part of our law from our early years as a nation, but it was not until 1970 that the Court finally held that it was an aspect of "due process" protected by the Fifth and Fourteenth Amendments to the Constitution. (p. 119)

Stevens then discusses, and quite rightly, the presumed infallibility of proof of guilt that could lead to unjust sentences, and chiefly the death sentence. The advances in DNA technology and forensic science have caused the release of many individuals sentenced to long terms in prison and execution, in which proof of guilt had been upended. Stevens notes, however:

> We may never know...that the risk of such injustice arises when a defendant is sentenced to death. Moreover, we also know that the risk is significant and that the finality of state action terminating the life of one of its citizens precludes any possible redress if a mistake does occur. (p. 122)

I am of two minds on this subject. An individual found guilty of <u>first degree</u> murder (and beyond the shadow of a doubt) has forfeited his own life. I do not see the justice in allowing him to live, even without chance of parole, but at taxpayer expense, so that he may indulge, while incarcerated, in activities his victims are no longer able to enjoy: pursuing hobbies, reading up on criminal law, body building in a prison gym, sports, and etc. Perfect justice would require that the criminal vanish as he made his victim vanish, and this would be communicated to him in no uncertain terms before his execution, with no mention of retribution by "society" or how his death would serve the interests of "crime deterrence."

On the other hand, because of the fallibility factor, I would support the idea of simply sentencing such an individual (together with the "vanishing" advisory) to life imprisonment in solitary confinement, but with none of the aforementioned amenities or indulgences. He would be incarcerated in a cell bare but for a bunk, a sink, and a commode, fed according to a prison's mess schedule, and left to his own mental devices until he rotted away. This also would amount to a "death row," but it would accommodate the very, very slim chance of a reversal of a court's conviction based on newly discovered skewed, quirky, manipulated, or false evidence.

Stevens ends this chapter with his proposed change to the Eighth Amendment:

> Excessive bail shall not be required, nor excessive fines imposed, nor cruel and unusual punishments *such as the death penalty* inflicted. (p. 123; *Italics* mine for Stevens's added words.)

Stevens saved the subjects of gun control and the Second Amendment for his last chapter, "The Second Amendment (Gun Control)." It is here that he begins to lose his measured calm and presence of mind. He claimed in an interview that it was the Sandy Hook Elementary School massacre in Newtown, Connecticut on December 14th, 2012, that prompted him to write *Six Amendments*. In his Prologue, Stevens claims that his discussion of the Second Amendment would be confined "to the area intended by its authors." This means that he will inject a bit of mind-reading and psychologizing about men who have been dead for over a century and a half. Never mind what they wrote. He includes a quotation from the late Chief Justice Warren Burger to telegraph his own feelings about guns and the presumed power of the government to regulate the private ownership of guns:

> Five years after his retirement, during a 1991 appearance on the *MacNeil/Lehrer NewsHour*, Burger himself remarked that the Second Amendment "has been the subject of one of the greatest pieces of fraud, I repeat the word 'fraud,' on the American public by special interest groups [e.g., he meant the National Rifle Association, or NRA] that I have seen in my lifetime."

(The *MacNeil/Lehrer NewsHour*, known since 2009 as the *PBS NewsHour*, is a "news" program of that BBC-wannabe, the Public Broadcasting Service, which in turn is "owned" by the Corporation for Public Broadcasting, which is affiliated with National Public Radio, both even bigger BBC-wannabes funded by taxpayer dollars and by "contributions from people like you.")

The Second Amendment reads:

> "A well regulated Militia, being necessary to the security of a free State, the right of the people to keep and bear Arms, shall not be infringed."

The Cornell University Law site provides a judicial history of the amendment and its varying interpretations.

> On the one hand, some believe that the Amendment's phrase "the right of the people to keep and bear Arms" creates an individual constitutional right for citizens of the United

States. Under this "individual right theory," the United States Constitution restricts legislative bodies from prohibiting firearm possession, or at the very least, the Amendment renders prohibitory and restrictive regulation presumptively unconstitutional.

On the other hand, some scholars point to the prefatory language "a well regulated Militia" to argue that the Framers intended only to restrict Congress from legislating away a state's right to self-defense. Scholars have come to call this theory "the collective rights theory." A collective rights theory of the Second Amendment asserts that citizens do not have an individual right to possess guns and that local, state, and federal legislative bodies therefore possess the authority to regulate firearms without implicating a constitutional right.

So, the phraseology, which is fairly clear – given the historical fact that states in the Framers' time depended on private citizens *who already owned guns* to become members of a militia – has been a bone of contention. One school of thought grants individuals the right to own guns; another denies that the Amendment grants that right.

To the contrary to Stevens's interpretation notwithstanding, the amendment grants private citizens to own guns. There are no extenuating circumstances, such as the kinds of guns, under which a federal or state government can prohibit private gun circumstances. The Cornell site records when the Supreme Court began to be unnecessarily fussy and "detail oriented":

In 1939 the U.S. Supreme Court considered the matter in *United States v. Miller*. 307 U.S. 174. The Court adopted a collective rights approach in this case, determining that Congress could regulate a sawed-off shotgun that had moved in interstate commerce under the National Firearms Act of 1934 because the evidence did not suggest that the shotgun "has some reasonable relationship to the preservation or efficiency of a well regulated militia . . . ." The Court then explained that the Framers included the Second Amendment to ensure the effectiveness of the military.

This is the interpretation with which Stevens agrees. As I remarked in my first column, "Justice Stevens's Liberty-Destroying Amendments":

> ...[I]n the video on the NRO site, George Stephanopoulos asks Stevens about the five words Stevens would add to the "amended" Second Amendment: "...the right of the people to keep and bear arms [*when serving in the militia*] shall not be infringed." (*Italics* Stevens's)

The "militia" meaning the National Guard or virtually any federal SWAT or armed law enforcement entity. It means that the government would have a monopoly on all weapons.....

> Stephanopoulos: "Do you think that....clearly...that was what was intended?"

> Stevens: "I do think that was what was originally intended, because there was a fear among the original framers that the federal government would be so strong that they might destroy the state militias. The amendment would merely *prevent arguments being made that Congress doesn't have the power to do what is in the best public interest.*"....

Have an argument that questions Congress's power to enforce gun-control? Stow it. Stevens's amendment forbids you to make it....

Stevens's amendment makes no sense at all. The right to bear arms *as a private citizen* either is or isn't "infringed." If it *is* infringed upon, then the only time you can exercise your "right" is when you're working for the government enforcing the government's will at gunpoint (lawfully or unlawfully). Then, when the task is completed, you would hand the weapon you used back to the armorer. You may "bear" the arms, but not own it.

If it *isn't* infringed upon, then you may own and "bear arms," certainly without leave of the authorities, and without having to serve in any government policing or military force. Period.

In the Framers' time, state militias were largely drawn from a population of *armed citizens*. Stevens can't have been ignorant of this fact. What the Framers had in mind when wording that amendment was not only the ability of states to protect their sovereignty from federal power (together with dealing with violence in a state), but also the ability of private citizens to protect themselves from federal and/or state power, as well. The Framers were thinking in fundamentals and far ahead to a possible future when the government would turn on its citizens. (See a history of Shay's Rebellion and Cliven Bundy's recent stand against federal authorities, for examples.)

In conclusion, Justice Stevens's book is a prescription for the expansion of federal power beyond what already exists. I'm certain of this: That if the Framers could be brought back to life to see the present scope of federal power, it would cause them to faint in an instance of mass aneurisms, whispering: "*What have you done???*"

Six Amendments: How and Why We Should Change the Constitution, by John Paul Stevens. New York: Little, Brown and Company/Hachette Book Group, 2014. 192 pp.

May 2014

الأمير سلطان الدين بن جاد بن حيد

ISLAM

The Ongoing Erasure of Europe

In a past column I discussed how the EU is obsessed with controlling the European's material existence. In this column the subject is how the EU is planning to control his spiritual existence.

The Gates of Vienna published a startling, translated column by German attorney Michael Schneider about an Organization of Islamic Conferences-approved (OIC) "framework" sponsored by the European Parliament, "which seems likely to be implemented across the EU. The proposed law would devise a draconian new form of politically correct 'tolerance' and impose it on European citizens and institutions by establishing bureaucratic bodies with the authority to enforce it."

The irony in the title of the proposed legislation was obviously lost on its authors, "A European Framework National Statute for the Promotion of Tolerance," for it is nothing but a blueprint for imposing across-the-board "intolerance."

Schneider opens his essay with:

> Anyone who speaks and writes about the abrogation of freedom in Europe is accused of being a pathological conspiracy theorist. So it is advisable to be a little more specific, and name names.

> The abrogation of freedom in Europe is not occurring naturally, but according to the planning of educated elites, who have been trained to replace civic freedoms — especially those of expression, of the press and of the airwaves — with ideological coercion, and thus smash civil society into microscopic shards, like valuable, defenseless porcelain.

Schneider writes that one of the chief culprits behind this legislation is a Professor Rüdiger Wolfrum, professor emeritus and one of the directors of the Max Planck Institute on foreign public law and international law in Heidelberg.

> This honorable person is also in a dubious think tank, "The European Council on Tolerance and Reconciliation" about which one may find relevant information on the homepage of the president of "The European Jewish Congress" (EJC), Viacheslav Moshe Kantor. Among other things are those documents which describe the political intentions of the think tank.

The subject document closes with a reference to that think tank:

> This text was prepared – under the aegis of the European Council on Tolerance and Reconciliation – by a Group of Experts composed of Yoram Dinstein (Chair), Ugo Genesio, Rein Müllerson, Daniel Thürer and Rüdiger Wolfrum.

The Three Expert Horsemen of the European Apocalypse? Surely. Throughout his essay, Schneider repeatedly refers to Wolfrum as "Wolfrum in Sheep's Clothing." And when you read the European Framework (in English) yourself, you will see that his sardonic contempt for the man is fully justified.

Of particular interest are paragraphs (a), (c) and (d) under Section 1: Definitions:

> (a) "Group" means: a number of people joined by racial or cultural roots, ethnic origin or descent, religious affiliation or linquisitc links, gender identity or sexual orientation, or any other characteristics of a similar nature.

> (c) "Hate crimes" means: any criminal act however defined, whether committed against persons or property, where the victims or targets are selected because of their real or perceived connection with – or support or membership of – a group as defined in paragraph (a).

> (d) "Tolerance" means: respect for and acceptance of the expression, preservation and development of the distinct identity of a group as defined in paragraph (a). The definition is without prejudice to the principle of coexistence of diverse groups within a single society.

Muslims, of course, would not be expected to abide by these rules. They can behead a British soldier in broad daylight in London and cite chapter and verse from the *Koran*, attack Jews in Malmo, rape as many Norwegian women as they like, and invade an auditorium and shout down any speaker who criticizes Islam, yet one may not take umbrage at their "religious affiliation" or ethnicity without risking the charge of having committed a "hate crime" and being "intolerant."

Muslims, however, can froth at the mouth in hatred and commit atrocious crimes, yet not be charged with "hate crimes." They can publicly demonstrate carrying signs that read "Freedom of Speech Go to Hell," "Islam Will Dominate," and "Behead Those Who Insult Islam" with impunity, yet anyone who appeared in public carrying a sign that read "Sharia Go to Hell" or "Islam is Barbarism" would soon be handcuffed by the police and led away to be charged with a "hate crime" and with "inciting violence."

Muslims are permitted to hate and express their intolerance. You, the non-Muslim, are not. "Respect, tolerate, and accept" the conundrum.

Schneider parses prominent sections of the European Framework law and explicates their meanings vis-à-vis EU-Speak. For example:

> The basic consideration[s] of the document as read are attractive and allow no suspicion to arise – that is if you do not know what EU political-speak means – for instance, "human diversity" standing for the systematic destruction of the autochthonic population and its traditional canon of values. **Whereas respect for human dignity is based on recognition of human diversity and the inherent right of every person to be different, etc. [Emphasis in bold is** Schneider's]

> All possible groups are supposed to be protected by this concept of tolerance — just not the majority population. With this policy, minorities are purposefully advanced at the cost of majority cohesion. This splits the society, thereby controlling it better and leading to the final goal. This becomes visible in the typical, EU-wide concept of the protected minority, which is inherently aimed at splitting the society — *divide et impera*:

In short – and because the chief beneficiary of this legislation will be Muslims – this means that the Muslim minority will be raised in status to that of the dominant Western culture. By effectively divorcing Muslims from secular Western society, and giving them a special, protected status, all the Dark Age practices inherent in Islam, including Sharia law, will be bestowed the same legal and moral status as the culture of the majority of non-Muslim Westerners.

However, the secular majority, in the name of "diversity," may not impose its values and ethics on the Muslim "minority" (that would be viewed as "oppression"), but the Muslim "minority" may chip away at the values and ethics of the majority in the name of "tolerance," until they disappear like the Titanic and slip beneath the waves of history.

The goals of Islamic "cultural" jihad have been iterated repeatedly, among which are the dissolution of Western civilization. The Muslim Brotherhood's strategy is clearly stated in an American court document that outlines how Islam will conquer the U.S. (and presumably Canada). That strategy can be seen at work in Europe, as well.

"The process of settlement is a 'Civilization-Jihadist Process' with all the word means. The Ikhwan [Muslim Brotherhood] must understand that their work in America is a kind of grand jihad in eliminating and destroying the Western civilization from within and 'sabotaging' its miserable house by their hands and the hands of the believers..."

Greece has gotten a head-start on the process. Atlas Shrugs reports that the Greek Supreme Court has held Sharia law superior to Greek secular or civil law.

> The last will and testament of a Muslim man, which was prepared according to Greek civil law, has been annulled in the Greek Supreme Court because it is not compliant with sharia law.

> Demeter Simeonidou, who was Muslim and lived in Thrace, wanted to leave all his assets to his wife. He prepared his will with this in mind under Greek law. But the will was challenged by Mr Simoenidou's sister who claimed that under Islamic law of succession, a Muslim does not have the right to make a public will and his assets must be distributed in accordance with sharia.

Simoenidou's sister is "different" because she believes in Sharia law. Her belief must be "respected," and to not respect it would be an insult and a denial of her "difference" and to rob her of her "diverse" status. To honor her late brother's will would by implication mean a derogation and defaming of Islamic law.

Schneider next turns to the notion of "group libel" (Section D, Definitions, [b]):

> ...defamatory comments made in public and aimed against a group as defined in paragraph (a) – or members thereof – with a view to inciting to violence, insulting the group, holding it to ridicule or subjecting it to false charges.

Schneider remarks:

Under such a totalitarian regime as planned here, Mohammed cartoons are just as unthinkable as are objective, scientific observations on any group having to do with its intelligence, its other genetic endowments, its behavior (unless it is described unreservedly positively) for instance, cumulatively occurring deviant or criminal behavior, etc. Even someone who reports that a group of sixty took part in the attack on a German police officer, and none of them was an ethnic German, can thus become a serious criminal. Warning: the persecution of the police officer is not the crime, but the politically incorrect report on it.

Sixty Muslims attacking the (presumably non-Muslim) German police officer would not be deemed a crime under the compromised German criminal code – that's just a "minority" protesting their victimhood by the "system" – but identifying the attackers as Muslim would be deemed a crime. Six Muslims gang-raping a non-Muslim woman or girl would not be judged a crime – that's just Muslims observing their religion, whose tenets may not be judged or held up in measure with secular law – but identifying the rapists as Muslim would be a crime.

Six ethnic Germans gang-raping an ethnic German woman or girl, however, is a crime that would fall under German secular law. But guess who would get the harshest sentencing under this schizophrenic code, and who would be left off with a slap on the wrist, even should a court dare such a rebuke?

Muslims may commit violence – Mohammad orders them to, it's in the *Koran*, that's something that can't be evaluated or judged – but a reporter who flouts the law of political correctness and identifies criminals as Muslims, would be found guilty of "inciting" violence or hatred or of intolerance or of insulting or defaming Islam and Muslims by having simply reported *facts*. But I don't think very many German or European reporters would face such a charge, once a nation adopted the European Framework legislation, because no newspaper or broadcast organization would ever hire them. The ones who might have would have been given pink slips.

In a spurt of thoroughness, lest anyone think he could critique the actions of Muslims in *the past* without risk of recrimination, there is this explanatory note:

> It must be understood that the "group libel" may appear to be aimed at members of the group in a different time (another historical era) or place (beyond the borders of the State).

Scholarly books on the pitfalls of Islam? Out of the question! TV specials on the bloody history of Islam from the 7th century on? Forget it! The history of Islamic slavery over the centuries, covering the deaths of millions of African blacks at the hands of Muslim slave traders to the kidnapping of approximately 1.5 million Europeans to die in servitude in North Africa or populate Muslim harems? Not a chance! Try and find a publisher. So what if the raiders of European coastal towns as far north as Iceland were pirates? They were Muslims, and their reputations are protected against "group libel." Recounting their actions would reflect "negatively" on the existing group, and that will not be allowed.

Next, Schneider highlights the consequences of creating a culture that is no longer Western but which has multiple personalities.

> To appease the critics, the unavoidable effect of the plan — splitting and ultimately destroying societies through the disproportionate demands of minorities who are impossible or difficult or unwilling to integrate — is concealed in an implausible formula: ***Promote tolerance within society without weakening the common bonds tying together a single society.***

Meaning that, hypothetically, German culture would simply be one of many "cultures" inhabiting the same nation, in the way of a placid mosaic, abiding peaceably with Islamic and other "cultures." Either Wolfrum and his colleagues are either ignorant of the fact, or choose not to mention it, but Islam "isn't in" Germany or any other European nation or in the U.S. to exist peacefully with non-Muslims, but to dominate, and that is what we have been witnessing in Europe for at least the last two decades. Muslims have been stating that intention from the beginning of their mass immigrations.

Schneider is certain that Wolfrum especially knows what he is doing.

As a proven legal thinker, he is not doing this by mistake but with malice aforethought and out of deepest conviction.

Schneider discusses how national and local governments would be expected to establish their own "special administrative units" that would police speech. He quotes from "Section 4: Limitations (f)":

> Freedom must not be used to defame other groups.

> Tolerance is a two-way street. Members of a group who wish to benefit from tolerance must show it to society at large, as well as to members of other groups and to dissidents or other members of their own group.

Absent in this incredible document is any mention of *individuals* or *individual right,* except incidentally in the preface. All rights, privileges and protections are calibrated to groups, to collectives. The string of "*Whereas*'s" in the beginning of the European Framework contains the basic premises of everything that follows and telegraphs the Framework's goals. For example,

> *Whereas* the concept of tolerance is the opposite of any form of unlawful discrimination....

Who is to decide what is "unlawful discrimination"? A special administrative unit.

> *Whereas* tolerance has a vital role in enabling successful coexistence of diverse groups within a single national society....[s]uch coexistence enriches and strengthens the fabric of the national society [and] should not affect the basic identity of that society or its shared values, history, aspirations and goals.

Good luck with that, because there is a catch.

> *Whereas* integration within a single national society *does not mean assimilation*....

> *Whereas* coexistence and cooperation within a democratic society require that individuals and groups make mutual concessions to each other....

Meaning that assimilation by Muslims into the larger Western society would not be imperative and wouldn't be a concession, but accommodation verging on assimilation by Westerners into Islamic culture would be imperative as a suicidal gesture of "tolerance" and "coexistence," which would be short-lived.

All in all, the whole European Framework document is deliberately calculated to produce a race reminiscent of the "pod people" from the film *The Invasion of the Body Snatchers*, with particular emphasis on transforming indigenous Europeans into obedient, unquestioning clones of each other, "tolerant" to the point of self-extinction and complicit in the destruction of European culture – that is, of the culture that once promoted freedom, freedom of speech, and their identities as Westerners.

After reading the entirety of this heinous document, I couldn't help but picture Wolfrum the co-author as the face on the screen of the classic Apple ad of 1984 that debuted the personal computer age, a disembodied face commanding adherence to a "garden of pure ideology...free from the pests of any contradictory true thoughts."

But where is the European athlete who will champion freedom of speech and hurl a hammer at the screen? Are Europeans nothing but "Ewes in Wolf's Clothing"? Well, no. There's Geert Wilders, Michael Stürzenberger, Elisabeth Sabaditsch-Wolff, and Lars Hedegaard, to name but a handful of Europeans ready to stake their all for freedom of speech and sound the alarm about the Islamic takeover of their continent. Their thoughts state the truth, yet they have been persecuted, prosecuted, and thrown to the wolves of Islam.

The same may be said about Michael Schneider, who also warns that that the alliance of the EU and Islam, if not exposed and stopped, will lead to the ultimate erasure of Europe by the hands of believers and the likes of Rüdiger Wolfrum and their dhimmified ilk.

Is America on the same path?

November 2013

The Incontrovertible Dead-End of Islam

Raymond Ibrahim, associate director of the Middle East Forum, recently published an article, "Offensive Jihad: The One Incontrovertible Problem with Islam," in the Middle East Forum and on *Pajamas Media* (October 30th). This excellent article for the first time (known to me, at least) addresses one of the fundamental problems of and with Islam I have always stressed: jihad. Jihad is a core tenet in what is a codified system of irrationalism that cannot be "reformed" without obliterating Islam as a distinct religious creed. Remove the belligerent jihadist commands from the Koran to wage jihad, for example, and it would cease to be Islam, not only in Muslim minds but in non-Muslim, as well.

There would, of course, remain a host of other irrational assertions and imperatives, such as the sanctioning of wife-beating and the murder of apostates and the like, which constitute, after some astounding mental gymnastics by Islamic clerics and scholars, chiefly the byzantine and illogical underpinnings of Sharia law.

The jihadist elements of Islam, however, are easily transmutable into a political policy, which is conquest of all non-Muslim or infidel governments and their submission to Sharia. That makes it an ideological doctrine. Muslims are either obliged to wage jihad, or they are not. Mohammad and Muslim scholars say they are. End of argument, so far as Koranic interpretation goes, and that interpretation is biased to the literal.

Reading the debates about what Islam's mission is and the role of jihad in it and what they truly "mean," I am always reminded of H.L. Mencken's observation on religious zealotry:

> "The urge to save humanity is almost always only a false-face for the urge to rule it."*

Islam is a puritanical creed that makes no allowances for either infidels or apostates or its adherents. I cannot believe that beneath the pious exterior of any person who would be seduced by Islam is not a seething, percolating envy of men who are indeed free, an envy easily and maliciously transfigured into violent jihad.

This policy is operative and underway today in Western nations with varying degrees of success, and it is making progress only by default. Islam is strong only because the West's defenders are emasculated by multiculturalist premises and a general disinclination to condemn any religion. Aggravating the problem is a repressed but general fear in the tolerance-obsessed and pragmatists of "offending" Muslims, who might start rioting and demonstrating again, claiming discrimination and disrespect, etc., none of it spontaneous but clearly organized and orchestrated by so-called "radicals."

I was initially impressed by Ibrahim's quotation from an entry on jihad in the *Encyclopedia of Islam*, which is an admission that "Islam must completely be made over before the doctrine of jihad can be eliminated" – until I realized that it could just as well mean that, after a global caliphate has been established, there would be no more justification for violent jihad. Every nation would by then be conquered, recalcitrant infidels slain, enslaved, or reduced to dhimmitude, and Sharia made the law of every land.

But, if Islam is completely "made over" in the sense of *reforming* it, what would be left of Islam that virtually any other creed could not claim as its fundamental tenets, as well? And to "make over" Islam, its principal font of "kilman" or wisdom, the objectionable and barbaric Mohammad, would need to be dispensed with. He is a role model for killers and tyrants and other psychopathic individuals. Remove that one critical link of the irrational and arbitrary in Islam, and all the links fall to the floor.
What would be substituted for Mohammad? It would need to be something as enduringly fable-worthy as Mohammad, but measurably benign. But, Islam has no alternative icons. What then, would be Islam's driving force, if not jihad as commanded by Allah as told to Mohammad?

Once Mohammad is removed from the text, the next step would be to question the existence and credence of Allah; if he commanded jihad, and if his word is sacred and unalterable, and known only through Mohammad, then he would need to be subjected to a "make over," much as the focus of Christian doctrine was shifted from an Allah-like Jehovah of the Old Testament to the largely pacific New Testament with Jesus Christ (as God on earth) and his homilies. If a "reformation" of Islam is undertaken, who in Islamic lore is Christ's counterpart? Would it be Abraham or Moses? But, neither of them was much better than

Mohammad in terms of their behavior towards men of other faiths; they also advocated the righteous slaughtering of unbelievers and sinners and distributing slaves, women, and sheep among their more zealous followers.

But, then, all faiths are faced with that intellectual chore regarding their own individual conceptions of a "supreme being," and not just Islam.

Ibrahim writes: "Worse, offensive jihad is part and parcel of Islam; it is no less codified than, say, Islam's Five Pillars, which no Muslim rejects." In sum, it is either-or: repudiate Islam entirely, or submit to the whole palimony of irrationalism that is Islam, including the imperative of jihad. The one incontrovertible problem with Islam (aside from the untenable claim of Allah's existence) is its dependence on violent conquest, or the initiation of force. This renders the creed absolutely *inconvertible* to a pacific doctrine. That is its unarguable dead-end.

Or, as Ayn Rand, the novelist/philosopher might have put it: "You can't have your mystic of muscle and deny him, too." He is either the source of Islam's potency, or he isn't. And if he isn't, whither Islam?

* *Minority Report: H. L. Mencken's Notebooks,* by Henry Louis Mencken. New York: Alfred A. Knopf, 1956. Entry 369, p. 247.

October 2010

The Incontrovertible Dead-End of Islam
Revisited

At the moment, I would rather be writing about the smiley mask that is falling from President Barack Obama and his tyrannical administration regarding the fabricated Benghazi "talking points," the Internal Revenue Service's targeting conservative and Tea Party groups for special attention, and the government's stealing the Associated Press's phone records. There is also the matter of the federal government stealing millions of personal health records in order to screen who will and will not be beneficiaries of Obamacare.

On top of all that, I learned that the Obama administration and the Mainstream Media are "like that." Imagine my index and second fingers crossed. For example, CNN vice president and deputy bureau chief Virginia Moseley is married to Hillary Clinton's deputy secretary, Tom Nides. CBS president David Rhodes is the brother of Ben Rhodes, master's degree holder in fiction-writing from NYU, Obama's deputy national security advisor, whose editing of the Benghazi "talking points" qualifies as fiction-writing. ABC president Ben Sherwood is the brother of special Obama advisor Elizabeth Sherwood. And, NBC was co-opted because its parent company is General Electric, which got $150 billion in stimulus money. What an incestuous extended family!

That leaves Fox News as the only other major news outlet that hasn't been co-opted or corrupted by the government. But there is one place Fox won't go, either: criticizing the Saudis. Fox is owned by Rupert Murdoch's News Group, which is about 10% owned by a Saudi royal prince.

The New York Times is completely liberal/left and shows no signs of wanting a reality check, so it can be written off. The same goes for the Washington Post, whose only saving grace is Charles Krauthammer's weekly column. Whether or not he's a neocon or merely a straight conservative, I've never been able to determine.

So, we don't need a 50-story pyramid housing Minitru in the middle of a squalid London in Orwell's *Nineteen Eighty-Four* to have a compliant propaganda entity. We have glitzy studio news sets and groomed talking head fashion plates and razzle-dazzle special effects to accomplish the same end: falsehoods and news reportage that is so biased it verges on fantasy.

That being said, I move on to another subject that must be raised, even though it is tangential to the foregoing vis-à-vis our foreign and domestic policies.

The following is a revised and expanded version of "The Incontrovertible Dead-End of Islam," which first appeared on October 30th, 2010. The revision and expansion are prompted by a May 13th, 2013 article by Daniel Pipes, president of the Middle East Forum, "Islam vs. Islamism," which also appeared in the Washington Times on May 13th. His article reflects a troubling central premise of alleging a necessary distinction between Islam and "Islamists," that is, between ordinary, non-violent Muslims and their violent, "extremist" or "radical" brethren.

Pipes opens with a reference to the Boston Marathon bombings of April 15th and the foiled attack on the Canadian rail link to the U.S.:

> What motives lay behind last month's Boston Marathon bombing and the would-be attack on a VIA Rail Canada train?

> Leftists and establishmentarians variously offer imprecise and tired replies – such as "violent extremism" or anger at Western imperialism – unworthy of serious discussion. Conservatives, in contrast, engage in a lively and serious debate among themselves: some say Islam the religion provides motive, others say it's a modern extremist variant of the religion, known as radical Islam or Islamism.

As a participant in the latter debate, here's my argument for focusing on Islamism.

His argument proposes a false dichotomy between Islam and "Islamists," that is, between Muslims who wage violent *jihad* on the West and even amongst themselves for sectarian reasons, and those who don't.

> Islam is the fourteen-century-old faith of a billion-plus believers that includes everyone from quietist Sufis to violent

jihadis. Muslims achieved remarkable military, economic, and cultural success between roughly 600 and 1200 C.E. Being a Muslim then meant belonging to a winning team, a fact that broadly inspired Muslims to associate their faith with mundane success. Those memories of medieval glory remain not just alive but central to believers' confidence in Islam and in themselves as Muslims.

Major dissonance began around 1800, when Muslims unexpectedly lost wars, markets, and cultural leadership to Western Europeans. It continues today, as Muslims bunch toward the bottom of nearly ever index of achievement. This shift has caused massive confusion and anger. What went wrong, why did God seemingly abandon His faithful? The unbearable divergence between pre-modern accomplishment and modern failure brought about trauma.

Muslims have responded to this crisis in three main ways. Secularists want Muslims to ditch the Shari'a (Islamic law) and emulate the West. Apologists also emulate the West but pretend that in doing so they are following the Shari'a. Islamists reject the West in favor of a retrograde and full application of the Shari'a.

These paragraphs astounded me. The first one glosses over the conquest of the Middle East and North Africa which necessitated forced conversion, butchery, and slavery. Remarkable military successes, indeed. But for their defeat at the Battle of Tours, the "Islamists" would have carved out a huge empire in Europe. What economic accomplishments? The period he cites spans the economically stagnant Dark Ages and early Western Medieval periods. Cultural successes? Other than a certain architectural style, translating some Aristotle and other ancient thinkers – whose works Islam subsequently rejected – I can't recall any great symphonies, artwork, or literature Islam produced in those six hundred years.

"Major dissonance" *within* Islam began over who was going to be Mohammad's official successor in the 630's. Thus the interminable conflicts between Sunnis and Shi'ites and other splintering sects of Islam. Islam never had any "cultural leadership."

Secularist Muslims may want Islam to ditch Sharia law but only at the risk of being deemed apostates and of their deaths. Apologist Muslims feign a hypothetical reconciliation between Sharia and Western concepts of freedom, and demand the incorporation of Sharia into Western law. "Islamists," however, are consistent with their creed, know that it *is* "retrograde" and primitive, and wage *jihad* to achieve that end.

Raymond Ibrahim, associate director of the Middle East Forum, on October 28, 2010, however, published an article, "Offensive Jihad: The One Incontrovertible Problem with Islam," also in the Middle East Form (October 28, 2010), which seems to be at fundamental odds with Pipes' article. Ibrahim's article addresses one of the fundamental problems of and with Islam, one which I have continually stressed: *jihad*. *Jihad* is a core tenet in what is a codified system of irrationalism that cannot be "reformed" without obliterating Islam as a distinct religious creed. Remove the belligerent *jihadist* commands from the *Koran* and *Hadith* to wage *jihad*, for example, and it would cease to be Islam, not only in Muslim minds but in non-Muslim, as well.

There would, of course, remain a host of other irrational assertions and imperatives, such as the sanctioning of wife-beating and the murder of apostates and the like, which constitute, after some astounding mental gymnastics by Islamic clerics and scholars, the byzantine and illogical underpinnings and text of Sharia law. The *jihadist* elements of Islam, however, are easily transmutable into a political policy, which is conquest of all non-Muslim or infidel governments and societies and their submission to Sharia. That makes it an ideological doctrine. Muslims are either obliged to wage *jihad*, or they are not. Mohammad and Muslim scholars say they are. End of argument, so far as *Koranic* interpretation goes, and that interpretation is biased towards the literal.

Reading the debates about what Islam's mission is and the role of *jihad* in it and what they truly "mean," I am always reminded of H.L. Mencken's observation on religious zealotry: "The urge to save humanity is almost always only a false-face for the urge to rule it." Islam is a puritanical creed that makes no allowances for either infidels or apostates or its adherents. I cannot believe that beneath the pious exterior of any person who would be seduced by Islam is not a seething, percolating envy of men who are indeed free, an envy easily and maliciously transfigured into violent *jihad*.

127.

This policy is operative and underway today in Western nations with varying degrees of success, and it is making progress only by default. Islam is strong only because the West's defenders are emasculated by multiculturalist premises and a general disinclination to condemn any religion. Aggravating the problem is an unadmitted but general fear in tolerance-obsessed pragmatists of "offending" Muslims, who might start rioting and demonstrating again, claiming discrimination, defamation, and disrespect, and etc., none of it spontaneous but clearly organized and orchestrated by so-called "radicals."

I was initially impressed by Ibrahim's quotation from an entry on *jihad* in the *Encyclopedia of Islam*, which is an admission that "Islam must completely be made over before the doctrine of *jihad* can be eliminated" – until I realized that it could just as well mean that, after a global caliphate has been established, there would be no more justification for violent *jihad*. Every nation would by then be conquered, recalcitrant infidels slain, enslaved, or reduced to *dhimmitude*, and Sharia made the law of every land.

In short, after all the killing, enslaving, and oppression, *jihad* would be *wrong!!*

But, if Islam is completely "made over" in the sense of *reforming* it, what would be left of Islam that virtually any other creed could not claim as its fundamental tenets, as well? And to "make over" Islam, its principal font of "kilman" or wisdom, the objectionable and barbaric Mohammad, would need to be dispensed with. He is a role model for killers and tyrants and other psychopathic individuals. Remove that one critical link of the irrational and arbitrary in Islam, and all the other links fall to the floor or dissolve into nothingness.

What would be substituted for Mohammad? It would need to be something as enduringly fable-worthy as Mohammad, but measurably benign. But, Islam has no alternative icons that meet that description. What then, would be Islam's driving force, if not *jihad* as commanded by Allah as told to Mohammad?

Once Mohammad is removed the text, the next step would be a "blasphemous" exercise and question the existence and credence of Allah; if he commanded *jihad*, and if his word is sacred and unalterable, and known only through Mohammad, then he would need to be subjected to a "make over," much as the focus of Christian doctrine was shifted from an Allah-like Jehovah of the Old Testament to the largely pacific New Testament with Jesus Christ and his pacifist homilies.

But Christ, to Islam, was merely an itinerant preacher, not a prophet. If a "reformation" of Islam is undertaken, who in Islamic lore would take Mohammad's place? Would it be Abraham or Moses? But, in the Old Testament, neither of them was much better than Mohammad in terms of their behavior towards men of other faiths; they also advocated the righteous slaughtering of unbelievers and sinners and distributing slaves, women, and sheep among their more zealous followers.

From where, then, would any "sacred word" come? Who would act as the incontestable vehicle of higher mysteries and moral diktats? On whose divine or temporal authority?

Ibrahim writes: "Worse, offensive *jihad* is part and parcel of Islam; it is no less codified than, say, Islam's Five Pillars, which no Muslim rejects." In sum, it is either-or: repudiate Islam entirely, or submit to the whole palimony of irrationalism that is Islam, including the imperative of *jihad*. The one incontrovertible problem with Islam (aside from the untenable claim of Allah's existence) is its dependence on violent conquest, or the initiation of force. This renders the creed absolutely *inconvertible* to a pacific doctrine. That is its unarguable dead-end.

Ibrahim goes to the nub of the conundrum that faces "moderate" critics of Islam:

> Worse, offensive jihad is part and parcel of Islam; it is no less codified than, say, Islam's Five Pillars, which no Muslim rejects. The *Encyclopaedia of Islam's* entry for "jihad" states that the "spread of Islam by arms is a religious *duty* upon Muslims in general ... Jihad must continue to be done until the whole world is under the rule of Islam ... Islam must completely be made over before the doctrine of jihad can be eliminated." Scholar Majid Khadurri (1909-2007), after defining jihad as warfare, writes that jihad "is regarded by all jurists, with almost no exception, as a collective *obligation* of the whole Muslim community."

129.

Even that chronic complainer Osama bin Laden makes it clear that offensive jihad is the root problem: "Our talks with the infidel West and our conflict with them *ultimately* revolve around one issue... Does Islam, or does it not, force people by the power of the sword to submit to its authority corporeally if not spiritually? Yes. There are only three choices in Islam... Either submit, or live under the suzerainty of Islam, or die."

Or, as Ayn Rand might have put it: "You can't have your mystic of muscle and deny him, too." He is either the source of Islam's potency, or he isn't. And if he isn't, whither Islam?

Andrew McCarthy, in his Family Security Matters article, "Obama's Betrayal of Islamic Democracy" (May 13th) remarks that it is difficult for "moderate" Muslims to "democratize" Islam: "As we have seen time and again, however, this is a very hard thing for moderates to do." McCarthy sympathizes with them.

It *is* hard for "moderate" Muslims to do because it would entail repudiating Islam altogether, and then they would no longer be "Muslims," moderate or otherwise. Islam is already a "democratic" system; once it attains hegemony wherever it reigns, that is pure "democracy" or majority rule in its original, unadulterated, and un-sweetened sense. Because "democracy" means "majority rule," that democracy would be represented by the Islamic *Ummah*, or the collective.

Is there such a thing as "moderate" Nazism, or "moderate" Communism? Or "moderate" totalitarianism? The "extremists" of Islam despise "moderate" Muslims because they know that Islam practiced consistently, that is, practiced root and branch, gives them political power. A "moderate" form of Islam, were such a thing possible, would deny them that power. A "moderate" form of Islam would be an emasculated form of it and no longer "Islam." The "extremists" or "radicals" know this, if the "moderates" don't.

Walid Shoebat, in his Pajamas Media column of May 18th,"Islam vs. Islamism: A Case for Wishful Thinkers," tasks Pipes, and, indirectly, McCarthy, as well, on not only the terminology of Islam vs. Islamism, but the core means and ends of Islam, which cannot be conveniently divorced from the ideology. After making hash of Pipes' statistical argument that not all Muslims condone violent *jihad*, and after citing Muslim authorities, dead and alive, on the legitimacy of *jihad* as central to Islam's existence, he quotes another authority on *jihad* and the establishment of a global caliphate by violence and stealth:

> What about Al-Ghazali, the famous theologian, philosopher, and paragon of mystical Sufism whom the eminent W. M. Watt describes as "acclaimed in both the East and West as the greatest Muslim after Mohammed, and he is by no means unworthy of that dignity"? Scholars like Pipes know the truth, yet completely ignore it. Al-Ghazali said:
>
> > *One must go on jihad (i.e., warlike razzias or raids) at least once a year... one may use a catapult against them when they are in a fortress, even if among them are women and children. One may set fire to them and/or drown them.... If a person of the Ahl al-Kitab [People of The Book—Jews and Christians, typically] is enslaved, his marriage is [automatically] revoked.... One may cut down their trees/...One must destroy their useless books. Jihadists may take as booty whatever they decide...they may steal as much food as they need.*

Shoebat writes that Pipes "even went as low to claim that Muhammad was a 'Muslim not an Islamist' and even distinguished him since, 'Islamism represents the transformation of Islamic faith into a political ideology.'"

By switching Muhammad from "Islamist" to "Muslim, Pipes must then answer a crucial question: Is Islam defined by its founder or by Mr. Pipes? Muhammad defined Islam as *"Al-Islamu deen wa dawla"* ("Islam is a religion *and* a state"). Pipes then must remove the "and" to substantiate his false case.

Islam is nothing if not a political ideology. The first time Mohammad raised his sword to forcibly convert men to Islam, and abandoned persuasion, that was the inauguration of political Islam. It has not changed since then. Force, coercion, slavery, death, and submission are the sole hallmarks of Islam.

The problem with Islam is that it is a religion. Religion is a primitive form of philosophy that explains existence and purports to give men a moral guide to living. Qua religion, it depends on faith in the existence of a supernatural being, and a form of altruism and collectivism, an altruism that is extended only to other Muslims and the collectivism of the *Ummah*. One could also argue that *jihad* represents a special kind of altruism: *Jihad* as seen as a vehicle of "salvation," with suicide bombers and plane hijackers acting as selfless and self-sacrificing drones to spread the word of Allah.

Allow me to pose this question: If one removed altruism and pacifism from Christianity, could one credibly call what was left "Christianity"? One could pose the same question about Judaism or Buddhism. Christianity, as a religion, it should be noted, has never been "moderated"; it has only been barred from acquiring political power. That was another unprecedented accomplishment of our Founders.

Pipes, dividing the discussion about Islam into three groups, writes that he belongs in the third group, which views "Islamism" as a "modern extremist variant of the religion, known as radical Islam or Islamism." He dismisses anyone who views Islam in its totality as succumbing to a "simplistic and essentialist delusion." This is an implicit disparagement of such survivors of Islam as Wafa Sultan and Ayaan Hirsi Ali, and of such champions against Islam as Geert Wilders. Treating Islam in its "totality" is as correct a way of treating it as it was of treating Nazism or Communism in their particular "totalities."

Those "totalities" are fundamentally, and incontrovertibly, *totalitarian*. There is no other way of looking at Islam, either.

May 2013

The OIC "Organizes" for Censorship

I begin this column with a quotation from Soren Kern's Gatestone article of December 11th, "OIC Blames Free Speech for 'Islamophobia' in West":

> The Organization of Islamic Cooperation, an influential bloc of 57 Muslim countries, has released the latest edition of its annual "Islamophobia" report.

> The "Sixth OIC Observatory Report on Islamophobia: October 2012-September 2013" is a 94-page document purporting to "offer a comprehensive picture of Islamophobia, as it exists mainly in contemporary Western societies."

> But the primary objective of the OIC—headquartered in Saudi Arabia and funded by dozens of Muslim countries that systematically persecute Christians and Jews—has long been to pressure Western countries into passing laws that would ban "negative stereotyping of Islam."

I've written in the past about the OIC's continuing campaign to insulate Islam from serious and satirical criticism here, here, and here in its call for international censorship. In this column I will discuss some angles Kern does not emphasize or discuss in his column.

The OIC report is unique in that it is illustrated and features photographs of individuals the OIC has found guilty of "Islamophobia," images of "offensive" newspaper headlines and photographs, and even of "defamatory" FaceBook pages and "tweets" that identify the alleged criminals. These can be found between pages 10 to 83, which constitute the bulk of the report and represent a "catalogue of crimes."

Kern writes, in reference to the OIC report:

> But the common thread that binds the entire document together is the OIC's repeated insistence that the main culprit responsible for "the institutionalization of Islamophobia" in Western countries is freedom of speech, which the OIC

133.

claims has "contributed enormously to snowball Islamophobia and manipulate the mindset of ordinary Western people to develop a 'phobia' of Islam and Muslims."

According to the OIC, freedom of expression is shielding "the perpetrators of Islamophobia, who seek to propagate irrational fear and intolerance of Islam, [who] have time and again aroused unwarranted tension, suspicion and unrest in societies by slandering the Islamic faith through gross distortions and misrepresentations and by encroaching on and denigrating the religious sentiments of Muslims."

"Freedom of expression" occurs six times in the document, while "freedom of speech" occurs only once. Not that it makes a difference which term the document employs. (Hillary Clinton would agree.) The term "hate speech" occurs fifteen times, while "hate crime" was used thirty-five times, most frequently in the "catalogue of crimes." The OIC demanded that Islam be "respected" seventeen times, and cited the importance of "interfaith dialogue" twenty-one times, even though such "dialogue" notoriously is set on Islamic terms and can go only one way, with concessions made by Christians and Jews, and none made by Muslims.

The term "toleration" and its variants, such as "intolerance," occur fifty-seven times in the document. What this means in practice is that Western societies must "tolerate" the depredations of Islam and "accommodate" Muslims at the price of Western civil liberties, while any resistance or criticism of Islam's ideology and practices, such as primitive Sharia law, can be designated as bigoted "intolerance."

Islamophobia, as Kern points out, is a "nebulous term" invented for the purpose of defaming the knowledge and certainty that Islam is primarily a political nemesis of totalitarian character and that Islam does *not tolerate* dissension from its tenets or the existence of other creeds.

According Robert Spencer and David Horowitz's 2011 publication, *Islamophobia: Thought Crime of the Totalitarian Future*:

> ...A front group – the International Institute for Islamic Thought – invented the term "Islamophobia.

Abdur-Rahman Muhammad is a former member of the International Institute for Islamic Thought. He was present when the word "Islamophobia" was created, but now characterizes the concept of Islamophobia this way: "This loathsome term is nothing more than a thought-terminating cliché conceived in the bowels of Muslim think tanks for the purpose of beating down critics." In short, in its very origins, "Islamophobia" was a term designed as a weapon to advance a totalitarian
cause by stigmatizing critics and silencing them.

The term occurs in the 1991 Muslim Brotherhood document, "An Explanatory Memorandum on the General Strategic Goal for the Group in North America," which details the means and ends of introducing Islam in the U.S. with the long-term end of colonizing it with immigrant Muslims and gradually and stealthily transforming it into an Islamic state. Kern quotes from the OIC report:

> Islam and Muslims have increasingly been portrayed as representing violence and terror that seek to threaten and destroy the values of Western civilization and that the Muslim way of life is incompatible with Western values of human rights and fundamental freedoms. For Muslims, Islamophobia is a deliberate scheme to distort the teachings and principles of peace and moderation engrained in Islam. As part and result of this scheme, Muslims tend to be collectively accused for any violence that erupts in society and are seen as ipso facto potential suspects well ahead of any investigation. This negative stereotype causes Muslims to be subjected to indignity, racial discrimination and denial of basic human rights. (p. 11, OIC report)

Islam and Muslims are justifiably associated with violence and terror and as a threat to Western civilization. That is, after all, an article of faith expressed in the Muslim Brotherhood memorandum of 1991.

> The Ikhwan [the Brothers] must understand that their work in America is a kind of grand Jihad in eliminating and destroying the Western civilization from within and "sabotaging" its miserable house by their hands and the

hands of the believers so that it is eliminated and God's religion is made victorious over all other religions.

And over all other ideologies, beliefs, and principles. There will be no arguing the point. Kern goes on about how that "grand jihad" is being carried out by calling for restrictions on speech that castigate or criticize Islam, and quotes from the report:

> The chapter further underscores that increased hate speech and discrimination against Muslims is a major factor behind the rise of the phenomenon of Islamophobia. In this context, acceptance of various forms of intolerance, including hate speech and the propagation of negative stereotypes against Islam and Muslims in some western countries contribute towards proliferation of intolerant societies. This process is further supported by three main manifestations, namely: the exploitation of freedom of expression and perpetuation of an ideological context advocating an inescapable conflict of civilizations; the right wing parties have politicized Islamophobia and instrumentalized fear in the context of growing socio-economic instability as well as the erosion of human rights in the name of national security and the fight against terrorism. (p. 7, OIC report)

The report claims that the news media is largely responsible for contributing to the alleged environment of fear and trepidation experienced by Muslims.

> ...the negative role played by major media outlets who not only propagate stereotypes and misperceptions about Islam, but also undermine and usually keep shadowed any meaningful instance of individuals or groups speaking out against intolerance, including advocacy of religious hatred and violence. This biased approach of the media has helped drawing an emphatically demonized, sometimes dehumanized, image of Muslims in the minds of a certain class of people which is predisposed to xenophobic feelings due to the increasingly dire economic situation, or the simply to the irrational fear of the other. (p. 15)

This is one of the most absurd claims of the report. The mainstream news media has not authored or perpetuated a "negative" stereotype of Islam and Muslims. Quite the contrary, it has instead largely white-washed Islam as a matter of editorial and journalistic policy, and denied that Islam has any causo-connection with Islamic terrorism, or has gone through evasive mental contortions to the same effect. If the news media has any "biased approach' to reporting news about Islam, it is in favor of Islam. One would need to search long and hard to find any major news media organization broadcasting any "negative" stereotypes or misperceptions about Islam.

Kern observes that:

> The OIC concludes that "journalists and media organizations have a responsibility to avoid promoting rhetoric of hate by acting as a platform for its widespread dissemination." (p. 30)

One supposes that the OIC's model news platforms are Qatar-funded Al Jazeera and Russia's government-funded RT (Russia Today).

Kern quotes two key paragraphs from the OIC report.

> According to the OIC, freedom of speech is to blame for the "perpetuation of Islamophobia," which:

> "...has become increasingly widespread, which, in turn, has caused an increase in the actual number of hate crimes committed against Muslims. These crimes range from the usual verbal abuse and discrimination, particularly in the fields of education and employment, to other acts of violence and vandalism, including physical assaults, attacks on Islamic centers and the desecration of mosques and cemeteries." (p. 11)

> "In this context, acceptance of various forms of intolerance, including hate speech and the propagation of negative stereotypes against Islam and Muslims in some western countries contribute towards proliferation of intolerant societies. This process is further supported by... the exploitation of freedom of expression and perpetuation of an

ideological context advocating an inescapable conflict of civilizations." (p. 7)

There is no mention in the report of the countless attacks on Christian churches or Jewish synagogues by Muslims. No mention in it of the countless physical attacks on Christians or Jews by Muslims. No mention of the murders committed by Muslims of non-Muslims. No mention of the countless rapes of non-Muslim women by Muslims in European countries. No mention of the nonstop, formulaic verbal abuse, libels, slanders, demonizations, and denigrations of Jews or Christians by Muslims in print or in person. No mention of the standard, stereotyping caricatures of Jews as drooling vampires by Muslims, or of the constant vilification of Jews as descendents of apes and pigs.

These are all "hate crimes" and instances of "hate speech" that go unpunished and unrecognized. But Islam is by *definition* the very "intolerant society" the OIC rails against with astonishingly arrogant verisimilitude, and in which, in Koranic theory and in practice, Muslims would be the only ones permitted "freedom of expression" in any way they chose with impunity.

Throughout the OIC report, Islam's "victimhood card" is as big as a highway billboard.

Kern also turns to the OIC's campaign in the United Nations to get its "tolerance" agenda approved and implemented.

> Chapter 4 of the report, "OIC Initiatives and Activities to Counter Islamophobia," focused on the OIC's ongoing efforts to promote the so-called Istanbul Process, an aggressive effort by Muslim countries to make it an international crime to criticize Islam. The explicit aim of the Istanbul Process is to enshrine in international law a global ban on all critical scrutiny of Islam and Islamic Sharia law.
>
> In recent years, the OIC has been engaged in a determined diplomatic offensive to persuade Western democracies to implement United Nations Human Rights Council (HRC) Resolution 16/18, which calls on all countries to combat "intolerance, negative stereotyping and stigmatization of… religion and belief."

And to prove that the U.N. knows and cares nothing about "human rights" (another "nebulous term"), look who was recently elected to be on its Human Rights Council:

> The General Assembly today elected 14 countries to serve on the United Nations Human Rights Council (HRC) for a period of three years beginning on 1 January 2014.
>
> Algeria, China, Cuba, France Maldives, Mexico, Morocco, Namibia, Saudi Arabia, South Africa, the former Yugoslav Republic of Macedonia, Viet Nam, Russia, and United Kingdom, were elected by secret ballot today at UN Headquarters in New York.

When you grant formal recognition to governments and régimes that are little more than secular or religious tyrannies, hereditary monarchies, totalitarian behemoths, and tin pot dictatorships, this is the caliber of absurdity and insanity one should expect. It's called political "diversity."

Finally, Kern turns to the OIC report's chief ends:

> Chapter 5 of the OIC report provides a set of conclusions and recommendations, which call on Western governments, international organizations and non-state actors to:
>
> "Take all necessary measures within their power and legal/jurisdictional systems to ensure a safe environment free from Islamophobic harassment... by strictly enforcing applicable hate crime and discrimination laws;
>
> "Create, whenever necessary, specialized bodies and initiatives in order to combat Islamophobia... based on internationally recognized human rights principles and standards;
> "Combat Islamophobic hate crimes, which can be fuelled by Islamophobic hate speech in the media and on the Internet;
>
> "Take all necessary measures to ensure that the media refrains from serving as a platform for the dissemination of hate speech... by associating extremism and terrorism to

Islam and Muslims… and presents the true positive nature of Islam.

"Implement provisions of UNHRC Resolution 16/18 through the Istanbul Process mechanism as it offers a positive platform for debate, exchange of best practices and maintaining of a common and unified stance." (pp. 37-38)

There's little humor to be found in the OIC report. But, on one hand, just before it "condemns in the strongest possible terms the reprehensible release of the film 'The Innocence of Muslims' as a deliberate incitement to hatred that has deeply offended more than 1.5 billion Muslims and all the people of conscience in the world" (p. 90; actually, it was just a trailer for the film, and I was offended more by its sophomoric amateurishness than by its content), the report noted that a "Ministerial *Brainstorming* [was] held during the 39th Session of the Council of Foreign Ministers, held in Djibouti in 2012…" On page 9, however, it was called a *barnstorming* session.

Kern ends his article with:

> The report concludes with the transcript of a speech by OIC Secretary General Ekmeleddin Ihsanoglu, in which he thanks American and European political leaders for their help (here and here) in advancing his efforts to restrict free speech in the West.

"The Istanbul Process initiated with Secretary of State Hillary Clinton and the EU High Representative for Foreign Affairs and Security Policy Catherine Ashton to build further on the consensus building that went into Resolution 16/18 must be carried forward. While the resolution forms a triumph of multilateralism, Istanbul Process must also be seen as a poster child of OIC-US-EU cooperation… I appreciate that this Process has come to be recognized as the way forward by all stakeholders… We need to build on it," Ihsanoglu said. (pp. 92-93)

Hillary Clinton, presidential hopeful, in December 2011 hosted an OIC "barn-or-brainstorming" session in Washington D.C. on how to curb freedom of speech without curbing freedom of speech. CNS observed that:

> The Obama administration says a meeting in Washington next week seeks to make progress in combating religious intolerance, but critics say the U.S. is pandering to an ideological agenda aimed at restricting speech critical of Islam.
>
> According to the State Department the aim is to find ways to combat religious hate without compromising freedom of expression. Detractors are skeptical that this can be done, and they suspect that free speech will end up the loser.

Hillary Clinton thinks that censorship is just *halal* when it comes to accommodating Islam and its 1.5 billion collect of brain-stultified manqués. She thinks that a semantic barnstorming stunt can be pulled off without actually censoring any and all criticism of Islam, serious or satirical.

However, remember what happened to the "Innocence of Muslims" fellow who she and Barack Obama blamed for the Benghazi attack during which four Americans were murdered...by Muslims. Even those responsible for the attack denied any connection of it with the video. The attack was in the works long before the video was broadcast on YouTube.

But, to Hillary, what difference does that make?

Are you Ready for Hillary in 2016? Prepared to shut your mouth and shut down your mind in the name of "tolerance"? She hopes Americans are ready to submit. She wants the White House very much.

She's "organized" her own brand of campaign *taqiyya*, but, the way things are going, that might not make a difference, either.

December 2013

The Psychology of Islamic Culture

It is commendable that someone should address the psychological profile of Muslims – that is, of individuals born into the culture of Islam – and Nicolai Sennels does that in his Jihad Watch article of October 30th, "Cultural psychology: How Islam managed to stay medieval for 1,400 years." I began reading it with some eagerness. Over the years I have had nothing good to say about the psychology or mindset of anyone who was either born into the religion/ideology and never challenged it or attempted to escape it, or who had been converted to it.

Sennels has studied Muslims prisoners in Denmark and has a wealth of insights to offer, one of which is that, from my perspective, at least, Islam provides a purported "moral" base which especially Muslim criminals justify or rationalize their criminal actions. The New English Review published his May 2010 study, "Muslims and Westerners: The Psychological Differences." I had already read that paper and discussed it in "Islam on My Mind" in May 2013.

Sennels' Jihad Watch summary, however, was disappointing. There were a number of statements in it with which I could legitimately quibble. Straight off, the very beginning of the article grated against my sensibilities. He began:

> While almost all other cultures changed from primitive and medieval to *democratic* and *egalitarian* societies, one culture managed to keep even its most brutal and backward traditions and values for 1,400 years until today. (*Italics* mine)

Sennels, apparently born and raised in socialist Denmark, might be forgiven for employing the highlighted terms. *Democracy* means "mob rule," or, the rule of the majority. What a majority may want and vote for is not necessarily rational or desirable by individuals who value their freedom to live their own lives unencumbered by a political or even the social consensus represented by majority rule. Numbers do not establish political or metaphysical truths.

A "democracy" is not what the Founders intended when they finished writing the Constitution. It was a rights-defending republic whose political structure was designed to stave off or frustrate all "democratic" legislation and collectivist popular sentiment. The American Constitution did not fail in that purpose. Its defenders in the person of our political leadership failed it.

Egalitarianism means the leveling of all to an ever-diminishing measure of "equality." Amendments IV, V and VI in the U.S. Constitution, for example, establish the "equality" of all men under the law, regardless of wealth or "social" status, and regardless of race, religion or gender. Egalitarianism, however, specifically aims to bring the best and the brightest, the ablest, and the exceptional down to a level of common mediocrity. Egalitarianism seeks to erase all measures of value, to reward the undifferentiated and the parasitical and to punish the distinguishable and the productive. One of egalitarianism's ends is to minimize "economic differences" to the point when there is more wealth in the looters' hands than in the hands of those from whom it was looted. This is called "social justice."

Egalitarianism is also altruistic. The most productive, the thrifty, and the virtuous living in an egalitarian society are expected to sacrifice themselves to the moochers, the spendthrifts, and the immoral. They are expected to defer to groups, gangs, and collectives acting in the name of the "public good," and to not complain when their lives have been abbreviated and their wealth expropriated or confiscated outright or by degree. This is the nature of such projects such as ObamaCare, in which the virtuous are expected to subsidize the medical insurance coverage of the least able, and to pay more for the "privilege."

The confusion about the meaning of *democracy*, and the benign misconstruing of *egalitarianism*, together have caused incalculable damage, which is why I have dwelt on those subjects here.

But, on to other reservations I have about his paper, keeping in mind that Sennels apparently is not well-versed in political philosophy.

Under the subheading of "Religion," Sennels writes:

> One main factor is that while all other religions allow their followers to interpret their holy scriptures, thereby making them relatively adaptable to secular law, human rights and

143.

individual needs, Islam categorizes Muslims who do not take the Quran literally as apostates. And according to Islamic law, the sharia, apostasy is to be punished with death. The Sharia thus makes it impossible for Islamic societies ever to develop into modern, humanistic civilizations.

Centuries of religious warfare in the West passed before Christian religions were diluted by Enlightenment ideas and subsequently leashed by secular law and forbidden to wage intramural *jihad* against members of opposing sects. Islam, however, as Sennels points out, cannot be leashed or similarly contained because its fundamental doctrine is one of conquest and submission.

Sennels under this same subheading reveals one contributing factor to the demonstrable irrationality of Islam and Muslims:

> Together with massive inbreeding – 70 percent of Pakistanis, 45 percent of Arabs and at least 30 percent of Turks are from first cousin-marriages (often through many generations) – this has resulted in the embarrassing fact that the Muslim world produces only one tenth of the world average when it comes to scientific research, and are dramatically under-represented among Nobel Prize winners. Fewer books have been translated into Arabic in the last thousand years than the amount of books translated within the country of Spain every year.

The inbreeding factor can account for the epistemological myopia of Muslims, particularly Muslim criminals. An inability to think, to project, to employ common syllogisms, to formulate one's own personal values (and not submit to those of the *Ummah* or the tribe) are all direct results of inbreeding.

Sennels published a revealing article on Muslim inbreeding in May 2013 on Islam vs. Europe, "Serious consequences of Muslim inbreeding." Among those consequences are lower average intelligence and impaired health.

> A rough estimate shows that close to half of the world's Muslims are inbred as a result of consanguineous marriages.

In Pakistan, 70 percent of all marriages are between first cousins – children of siblings – and in Turkey the share is 25-30 percent.

Statistical research on Arabic countries indicates that up to 34 percent of all marriages in Algeria are blood-related as are 46 percent in Bahrain, 33 percent in Egypt, 80 percent in Nubia (the southern part of Egypt), 60 percent in Iraq, 64 percent in Jordan, 64 percent in Kuwait, 42 percent in Lebanon, 48 percent in Libya, 47 percent in Mauritania, 54 percent in Qatar, 67 percent in Saudi Arabia, 63 percent in Sudan, 40 percent in Syria, 39 percent in Tunisia, 54 percent in the United Arabic Emirates and 45 percent in Yemen. According to Dr. Nadia Sakati of King Faisal Specialist Hospital in Riyadh, 45 percent of married Arab couples are blood-related. The fact that many of these couples are themselves children of blood-related parents increases the risk of negative consequences.

Sennels reaches some disturbing conclusions that connect Muslims with terrorism.

The consequences of consanguineous marriages may also bring us closer to an understanding Islamic terrorism. One study suggests that many suicide bombers are suffering from depression. Among some Muslims their actions are considered a socially acceptable way of committing suicide in order to end mental torment.

Being physically handicapped or mentally retarded often leads to exclusion. Becoming a martyr may be the only chance of achieving social recognition and honor. Some cases of Down's syndrome may be another unpleasant effect of inbreeding and al-Qaeda has been known to use people afflicted with it. People with low intelligence may also be more easily convinced that Islam, with its promise of 72 virgins to Muslims who die fighting for their religion, is true.

To return to the subject of Arabic translations of books:

Fewer books have been translated into Arabic in the last thousand years than the amount of books translated within the country of Spain every year.

Among those fewer books has been a translation into Arabic of Adolph Hitler's *Mein Kampf*, precisely because of its virulent antisemitism and because the Nazi worldview is copasetic with the Islamic worldview. Only the "races" have changed, that is, Hitler trumpeted the racial superiority of the Germans, while Islam trumpets the superiority of Islam . Victor David Hanson noted as long ago as September 2006, in his article, "The Waiting Game: Do We Really Need Further Convincing of the Threat We Face?" that:

> Hezbollah's black-clad legions goose-step and stiff-arm salute in parade, apparently eager to convey both the zeal and militarism of their religious fascism. Meanwhile, consider Hezbollah's "spiritual" head, Hassan Nasrallah — the current celebrity of an unhinged Western media that tried to reinvent the man's own self-confessed defeat as a victory. Long before he hid in the Iranian embassy Nasrallah was on record boasting: "The Jews love life, so that is what we shall take away from them. We are going to win because they love life and we love death."

> Iran's Mahmoud Ahmadinejad trumps that Hitlerian nihilism by reassuring the poor, maltreated Germans that there was no real Holocaust. Perhaps he is concerned that greater credit might still go to Hitler for Round One than to the mullahs for their hoped-for Round Two, in which the promise is to "wipe" Israel off the map.

> The only surprise about the edition of Hitler's *Mein Kampf* that has become a best seller in Middle Eastern bookstores is its emboldened title translated as "*Jihadi*" — as in "My Jihad" — confirming in ironic fashion the "moderate" Islamic claim that Jihad just means "struggle," as in an "inner struggle" — as in a *Kampf* perhaps.

Under the subheading of "Child rearing" in his Jihad Watch article, Sennels describes the method by which Muslim children are browbeaten into obeying and following the rituals and "truths" of Islam, a scare tactic not so dissimilar from what I experienced growing up in a strict Catholic household. He writes:

> Together with the wide use of violence and even torture within Muslim families, the horrific amount of daily family executions of Muslim youth, this is enough to keep the vast majority from even considering escaping the way of the Sharia. The Qur'an's and the Hadiths' many promises of hellfire to those who go against Muhammad's orders and example scares many from leavin the culture that bring them so much suffering.

Precisely. My own childhood thoughts on the matter were: If you need to frighten me into being a "good" Catholic, where is the moral argument? For example, watching on TV the various productions of Charles Dickens' *A Christmas Carol* in my formative years, when I witnessed Scrooge being terrorized into becoming a "virtuous" man, simply buttressed my conclusion that there was no moral argument other than "we say so, and take it on faith." So I can imagine how fearful a Muslim would be to question the "say so's" of his imam, mullah, or the Qur'an.

Fear of retribution may be one factor contributing to a rank-and-file Muslim's reluctance to question his "faith." Delving a little more deeply into that psychology, I would think that it is more a matter of being comfortable with an ideology/religion that makes no demands on one's mind. All one need do is conform to the rituals and strictures and one is left is alone.

Under the subheading "Ethnic pride," Sennels drops the ball and does not elaborate on the fact that Islam is not a "race," but an ideology. I'm sure he realizes this, but it would have helped if he had mentioned it in passing. There are Arabic, Asian, black, Caucasian (converts), Chinese, and Indian and Pakistani Muslims, to name but a few ethnic or national groups.

> Another cultural psychological factor enabling Islamic culture to remain unchanged in a globalised world with all its possibilities concerns Muslims' ethnic pride. No matter how ridiculous or embarrassing it may seem to the outsider, most Muslims are proud of being Muslim and a follower of Islam.

According to Islam they are destined to dominate the rest of us, and we are so bad that we deserve the eternal fire.

Muslim spokesmen charging critics of Islam with "Islamophobia" imply or state directly that such a phobia is "racist." Too many Westerners fall for the fallacy and join in the wolf-pack howling to punish "Islamophobes," whether they write cogent books critical of Islam or leave a pig's head on the doorstep of a mosque. It makes no difference to the pitchfork-and-torch mobs.

Without quibbling about when the Dark Ages ended and the Medieval and Enlightenment eras began, Islam is product of the Dark Ages, of the 7th century, an enemy of knowledge, enlightenment, and freedom – if the Dark Ages can be described as a period in human history when superstition, ignorance, and slavery governed human existence.

Also, I don't know if many Muslims can say that they are "proud" of being Muslim. If there is any emotion at all, one can't imagine that it is anything other than a seething, repressed resentment of anyone who is not a Muslim, that is, of anyone who is not committed to a set of primitive rules that govern his existence and prohibit any kind of meaningful happiness. Pride, after all, implies a *self* that can take stock of one's virtues and one's relationship with existence and with other men. Islam, however, does its best to erase the notion of "self" from one's existence.

Islam is anti-life, anti-mind, anti-value, and anti-man. That is why it has been able to remain unchanged for 1,400 years. Its chief "strength" is its nihilistic nature, proof against all thought and life-affirming values. And there are just too many people – namely, Muslims – willing to surrender their minds to the suffocating comfort zone of "authority." Muslims don't have a corner on that "original sin" – the refusal to think – but their totalitarian ideology is an immediate peril to those who do choose to think. I can't say I'm the first to say it: Islam *is* a mental illness. That's its fundamental psychology, the debilitating and crippling legacy of its founder transmitted through fourteen centuries of Muslim madness to its contemporary spokesmen, leaders, and rank-and-file.
The illness, however, is no defense against Islam's essential criminal character.

November 2013

A Diagram of the Islamic Beachhead in the U.S.

The Muslim Brotherhood has established roots in America perhaps greater and deeper than the espionage and covert activist organizations of Nazi Germany and Soviet Russia. It would be instructive to include a graphic illustration of that beachhead. And the purpose of that organization is in complete conformance with the Brotherhood's stated agenda: To first corrupt the cultural, social, and judicial foundations of the country by "stealth jihad." Then, to make Sharia the law of the land. The central organization happens to be the Council on American-Islamic Relations (CAIR). All of the organizations illustrated in the diagram are either direct affiliates of the Brotherhood, or are indirectly related and interlinked.

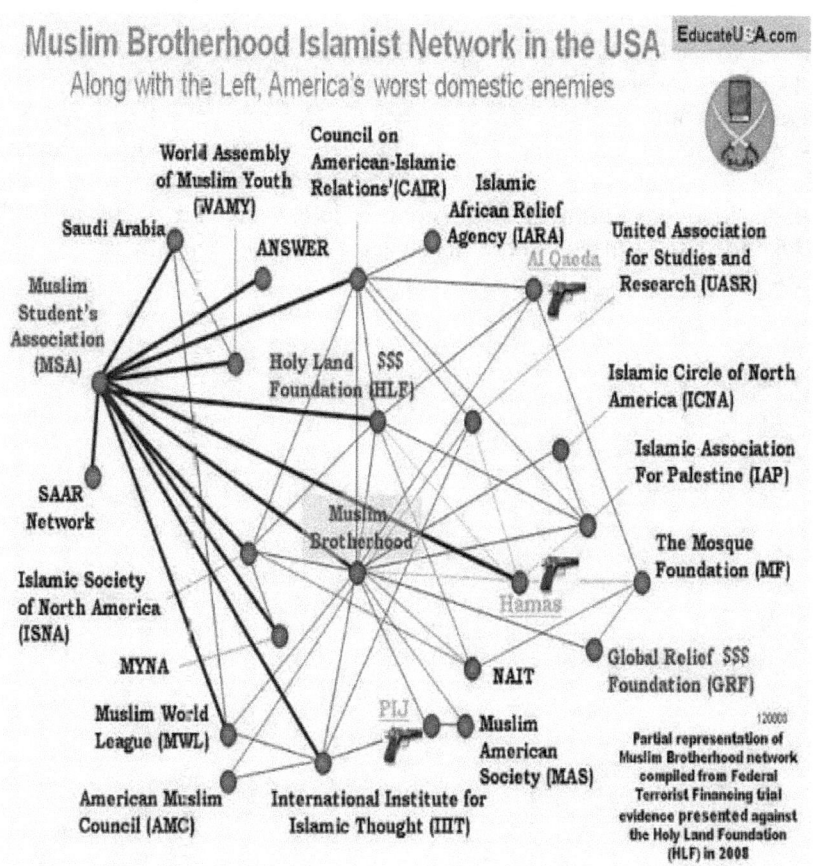

1) Council on American-Islamic Relations (CAIR)
2) Council of Islamic Organizations of Greater Chicago (CIOGC)
3) Islamic Circle of North America (ICNA NY and Canada)
4) Islamic Council of New England (ICNE)
5) Islamic Organization of North America (IONA)
6) Islamic Society of North America (ISNA)
7) Justice For All
8) DawaNet
9) Majlis Shura of Atlanta
10) Michigan Muslim Community Council
11) Muslim Alliance of North America (MANA)
12) Muslim Public Affairs Council (MPAC)
13) Muslim Ummah of North America (MUNA)
14) Muslim Leadership Council of New York and Muslim Peace Coalition

There are also Islamic lawyers' medical associations. About 70% of the over 2,200 mosques in the U.S. preach the Wahhabi version of Islam, which, among other things, means active *jihad* against the U.S. A USA TODAY article of February 29th, 2012, reported that "while protests against new mosques in New York, Tennessee and California made headlines, the overall number of mosques quietly rose from 1,209 in 2000 to 2,106 in 2010." Further, there are at least a dozen Muslim camps that train Muslims for violent *jihad*.

May 2014

BOOKS

Book Review: *Fear Itself*

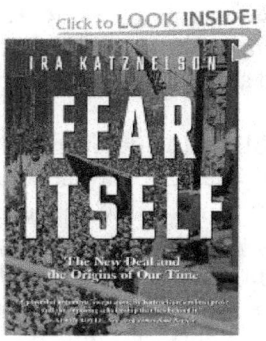

"So, first of all, let me assert my firm belief that the only thing we have to fear is fear itself—nameless, unreasoning, unjustified terror which paralyzes needed efforts to convert retreat into advance." – Franklin D. Roosevelt, first inaugural address, 4 March 1933.

The standard interpretation of this inane statement is that we shouldn't allow our fears to overcome a commitment or determination to act. This was a tidewater year for the Progressives, who wanted to turn their "retreat" into an "advance." Roosevelt was their political point man, and a host of economists and academics acted as his "bandstand" backup chorus. A literal construction of the statement is:

> We shouldn't allow a knowledge of the consequences of our proposed statist policies to stop us from enacting those policies. Whether or not those policies accomplish their ends, it is important that we "advance" and not be terrified of the certain outcome. We shouldn't be afraid of turning the country into a fascist/socialist slave state. It is for the "public good," and the "public good" justifies any action the state may take to secure it. If that means abrogating, rescinding, or abridging individual rights, if that means crippling the

economy, and redirecting Americans' wealth and efforts in a more public-spirited direction, so be it. We must all pull together. Anyone caught slacking at his oar, or mumbling against the whip-wielding overseers, will be isolated, vilified and punished. Possibly even tossed overboard.

Never mind that it was the federal government's fiscal policies that caused the Depression and perpetuated it. More "needed efforts" are imperative to convert a free country into a minimum security prison.

A new book has been published which partly explains why today we are burdened with an arrogant federal government (and its state-sized copy cat minions), one endlessly expanding the scope of its powers, *Fear Itself: The New Deal and the Origins of Our Time*, by Ira Katznelson.* Katznelson is Ruggles professor of political science and history at Columbia University, president of the Social Science Research Council, and research associate at Cambridge University's Centre for History and Economics. He is a dyed-pink Progressive and liberal and advocate of precisely the welfare state and command economy we are enduring today. His book covers the beginning of the New Deal up to the election of Dwight D. Eisenhower in 1952.

The Progressive – read socialist – antecedents of The Social Science Research Council (SSRC) are impeccable. A Wikipedia account of the SSRC names many of the usual suspects. Founded in 1923,

> To support its work, the SSRC turned not to the U.S. government, whose support seemed more appropriate for the natural sciences, but to private foundations. For the first fifty years, well over three-quarters of the SSRC's funding was provided by the Russell Sage Foundation, the Ford Foundation, the Carnegie Corporation, and two Rockefeller philanthropies, the Laura Spelman Rockefeller Memorial and the Rockefeller Foundation.

> The SSRC was part of a wider Progressive Era movement to develop organizations of expertise that could dispense disinterested knowledge to policymakers. These organizations would tap leading thinkers in various fields to think creatively about how to rid the nation of the social and political ills brought on by the Industrial Revolution.

152.

The knowledge gathering was not so "disinterested" – it was knowledge collected to "prove" the necessity of a planned economy and a regimented society. And the "ills" of the Industrial Revolution were inherited from conditions prevalent in the pre-Industrial Revolution. If there were any societal "ills" left once the Revolution got into full swing, they were a consequence of statist policies in America and in Europe.

But, enough of focusing on the ideological familiars of Progressivism. Katznelson's book, while a friendly and commodious history of the New Deal's origins at a daunting 720 pages, focuses on one aspect of the New Deal and FDR's policies: the Democratic Party and its continuing tradition of racism. He makes a very strong and credible argument that FDR's New Deal and its swollen progeny were largely made possible by members of Congress, especially from the southern states, who were outspoken racists and who were able to "whip" the votes to pass New Deal legislation. It was a *quid pro quo* trade-off, a matter of horse-trading and logrolling between the executive and legislative branches of government.

In short, FDR and his brain trust wanted to pass welfare state legislation and economic controls over the whole nation. The southern states wanted to preserve their Jim Crow legal structure and societies from interference from Washington, under the guise of "states' rights." The southern states controlled the voting blocs in the Senate and House. The arrangement was amenable to both sides as long as no one paid it much attention. FDR did his best to scratch the backs of vociferous bigots in Congress, and the bigots scratched his back and surrendered the right of their states to remain economically independent from Washington.

The Democratic Party has a history – nay, nearly a tradition – of racism and keeping blacks on the federal plantation of dependency and electoral servitude. Ronn Torossian, in his April 14th FrontPage article, "The Racist, Discriminating Democratic Party," reminds us that:

> The Republican Party was born just prior to the Civil War for the sole purpose of combating slavery and it fought against the party of slavery. The Republican Party is the party of freedom and economic liberty and prosperity – as it was then and now. The Democratic platform of the 1860s was a pro-slavery policy that sought to keep people

153.

enslaved. In the 1950s and 1960s, the Democratic Party was the enforcer of "Jim Crow" laws and segregation. In 1964, there was a filibuster of the Civil Rights Act by Democrat Senator Robert Byrd (D-WV) which lasted 14 hours. The Act was crafted and supported by a vast number of Republicans in the Senate, while opposed by southern Democratic senators (including Al Gore Sr).

I wouldn't go so far as to claim that the Republicans are still pro-freedom. I doubt very much they know anymore what they ought to be *for*. And the Civil Rights Act *is* a usurpation of the right of free association and assembly. In a truly free country, racists and bigots would be marginalized and not fare well, either socially or economically. However, this much is true:

> Today, the Democrats continue to keep people in place and pursue centralized government, as a further way for more government control, particularly over the poor. The Democratic Party seeks to tell people how to eat, raise their families, and in this administration, how to have healthcare.

And the coin has been reversed since Senator Byrd and George Wallace's hegemony. Now it is black Congressmen and white-guilt liberals who dominate the Democratic Party.

Katznelson's book is an unapologetic *apologia* for how the current federal behemoth came into being. To his credit, he pulls no punches while discussing not only how FDR was able to get his statist legislation passed and implemented with the help of southern politicians, but why the arrangement also contributed to the U.S. making the totalitarian Soviet Union its chief ally during World War II, with Roosevelt and his political allies knowing full well the brutal truth about the Soviet Union: that it was a dictatorship with the blood and deaths of millions on its hands.

Katznelson's thesis, which he thoroughly documents throughout (there are 181 pages of lengthy end notes), is that:

> The South was singular. There, a racial hierarchy and the exclusion of African-Americans from the civic body were hardwired in law, protected by patterns of policing and accepted private violence, which created an entrenched

system of racial humiliation that became everyday practice…

…[T]he farther South one went in the United States, the greater the influence in shaping the content of the New Deal. We will discover the central role played by the once-slave South in Congress, where representatives from the seventeen states mandating racial segregation were pivotal members of the House and Senate. Democrats, nearly to a person, they were the most important "veto players" in American politics. Both the content and the moral tenor of the New Deal were profoundly affected. Setting terms not just for their constituencies but for the country as a whole, these members of Congress reduced the full repertoire of possibilities for policy to a narrower set of feasible options that met with their approval. No noteworthy lawmaking the New Deal accomplished could have passed without their consent. Reciprocally, almost every initiative of significance conformed to their wishes. (pp. 15-16)

Katznelson describes the ""question" faced by Roosevelt and his political allies of how to rescue the country from the government-perpetuated Depression but at the same time "save" capitalism:

During the period from the rallying call by the new president to confront fear itself on March 4, 1933, to the Nazi invasion of Poland six years later [in September, 1939; Katznelson omits mention of the co-invasion of Poland by the Soviets two weeks later, per the Molotov–Ribbentrop Pact], the New Deal was concerned, above all, with questions of political economy. Could capitalism be rescued? On what terms? With what degree of public support? The core policymakers in this initial phase of the New Deal never thought the USSR or Nazi Germany could provide workable models. But they were drawn to Mussolini's Italy, which self-identified itself as a country that had saved capitalism….

Desperate for tools and itself in an experimental mood, the Roosevelt administration in the 1930s did not so much

155.

adopt a pro-Mussolini stance as seek to associate with Italian Fascism, of course on American terms for America's own purposes, seeking to find policy models that could be put to use under democratic conditions. (pp. 92-93)

So much for the "grand" vision enunciated by FDR. His agenda was clear, but how to follow it remained a coin toss. The PR image of FDR as a walking vehicle of wisdom and perfect solutions is a lie. He was a pragmatist looking for a way to "save" capitalism by fitting it into the least offensive chains available. He looked abroad for answers.

And when the U.S. entered the war against Nazi Germany and Imperial Japan, suddenly the Soviet Union became a "workable model" of an ally. The heinous Soviet policies of starving millions, incarcerating untold numbers of Russians in Gulags, a secret police rivaled in its brutality only by the Gestapo, the show trials, were all forgotten. FDR wished Americans to forget what they knew about Stalin and the nature of his Communist dictatorship – much as Barack Obama wishes Americans to forget what the Muslim Brotherhood is and represents. Katznelson does not dwell on that subject, either. For a description of how duplicitous FDR was about our relations with the Soviet Union, see Diana West's *American Betrayal: The Secret Assault on Our Nation's Character*.

By 1945, the Roosevelt/Truman New Deal administrations had learned how to get things done. They emulated Otto von Bismarck and established the country's first permanent welfare state program:

> On August 14, 1935, the president signed the historic Social Security Act. By establishing federally managed old-age pensions and unemployment insurance, it considerably altered the contours of America's labor markets....(p. 258)

Katznelson argues that on the surface, the cooperation of the southern states was not crucial to the passage of the Act; however, southern blocs in the House and Senate deliberated on key elements of the Act at critical junctures in the legislative process, and allowed it to move ahead to the White House.

> ...Social Security was approved nearly without opposition by crushing bipartisan votes of 77-6 in the Senate and 372-33 in the House...

> A crucial vote to recommit the bill to the House Committee on Ways and Means attracted all but one Republican. The amendment failed, 149-253, because southern Democrats stuck with the party position, voting at a high level with fellow Democrats. Had the 141 Democrats in the chamber from the seventeen southern states resisted the legislation, it well might not have passed. (pp. 259-260).

After Roosevelt died in 1945, the "spirit of Yalta" evaporated and relations between the U.S. and the Soviet Union chilled. National security became the watchword in Washington. However, again, the definition of national security depended on the perceptions and cooperation of the southern "Jim Crow" states.

> Faced with insecure support from the left side of his party and with complex divisions among Republicans, Truman and his administration came to rely heavily on southern legislators, especially in congressional committees and, where needed, on the floor of each chamber, to lead coalitions that would advance their preferred policies. The policy steadiness, seniority, and party leadership of southern representatives placed them in a pivotal role when the content of national security bills was crafted, when the amending process had to be controlled, and when votes had to be won when there were divisions on the floor. (pp. 425-426)

From the very beginning of his terms as president, FDR and his advisors cast about for some "middle ground" between the fiat power necessary to advance the Progressive cause and checks and balances enumerated in the Constitution, and some way to preserve freedom by diminishing it and seeming to be champions of "democracy." But there were those who had FDR's ear who had no illusions about what was necessary to implement an American version of Fascism.

Writing a series of widely noted articles for The New Republic under the rubric of "A New Deal for America," the economist Stuart Chase offered "a survey for a third road" between violent Fascist or Communist revolution...and a "business dictatorship" whose road...has mud holes and soft shoulders." He called for a "third and last road," a path that "may entail a temporary dictatorship," though one that "will not tear up customs, traditions and behavior patterns to any such extent as promised by the Red or the Black dictatorship." (p. 118)

Walter Lippmann, the arch-Progressive journalist and political commentator who nurtured a contempt for the "public" *and* Constitutional principles (remind you of the current president and his Attorney General? In his 1925 book, *The Phantom Public*, he argued that Americans should be governed by a self-perpetuating elite of "insiders") was more forthright about what he thought was necessary to correct the doldrums that America was experiencing. In a series of columns about the Depression and the ongoing economic crisis in the New York Herald Tribune in January and February 1933, before FDR took office in March, he opined:

"The situation," he wrote, "requires strong medicine." In advocating a grant of "extraordinary powers" to the incoming president, he insisted that "the danger we have to fear is not that Congress will give Franklin D. Roosevelt too much power, but that it will deny him the power he needs. The danger is not that we shall lose our liberties, but that we shall not be able to act with the necessary speed and comprehensiveness." Extraordinary authority, he proposed, should give the president, "for a period say of a year, the widest and fullest powers under the most liberal interpretation of the Constitution." (p. 118)

"Temporary extraordinary powers" granted to any nation's executive as a rule become set in cement and are permanent. After all, there is no warranty guarantee on the length of a crisis. Ask Rahm Emanuel. Katznelson continues to quote Lippmann without flinching:

Concurrently, Congress should "suspend temporarily the rule of both houses, to limit drastically the right of amendment and debate, to put the majority in both houses under the decisions of a caucus." (p. 118)

That would work. After all, when Hitler took power late in January 1933, he persuaded the Reichstag late in March to cease functioning as a parliamentary entity with the <u>Enabling Act</u>. The "temporary" cessation of Germany's parliament became permanent. Lippmann was proposing that Congress gag itself.

> This supersession of normal politics, he concluded, "is the necessary thing to do. If the American nation desires action and results, this is the way to get them." Lippmann directed the same advice to his good friend, the president-elect. During a February 1 visit to Warm Springs, Georgia, he counseled how "the situation is critical, Franklin. You may have no alternative but to assume dictatorial powers." (p. 118-119)

Lippmann deemed necessary the suppression of normal politics – read individual rights and the rule of law. Roosevelt was all too agreeable to assume dictatorial powers. The only thing he likely feared was that Congress would not consent to gagging itself and placing its functions under the thumb of a caucus of a pro-Roosevelt clique.

Katznelson then proceeds to eulogize Roosevelt's inaugural address.

> [Roosevelt] went on to voice confidence that it would be possible to find a way within the Constitution of the United States to respond effectively. "Our Constitution is so simple and practical," he reassured with a high degree of ambiguity, "that it is possible always to meet extraordinary needs by changes in emphasis and arrangement without loss of essential form."....

> Should Congress not act promptly and decisively, [Roosevelt] warned, "I shall not evade the clear course of duty that will confront me. I shall ask Congress for the one remaining instrument to meet the crisis – broad Executive power to wage a war against the emergency, as great as the power that would be given to me if we were in fact invaded by a foreign foe." (pp. 121-122)

We can all remember how <u>Chief Justice John Roberts</u> changed the "emphasis" and rearranged the Constitution when he upheld Obamacare, without losing the Constitution's "essential form." However, remove the engine from a car, and the car has not lost its "essential form." But it is otherwise powerless and useless.

The powers Roosevelt was asking for were hardly "ambiguous." Failing to get the cooperation of Congress, he wanted it to allow him to declare war on the domestic crisis. Sound familiar? How many "wars" have been declared on something or other by Congress, the federal government ,and the White House since then? On drugs? On obesity? On smoking? On guns? On crime? On Wall Street? On poverty? On racism? On crime itself? The crises have never ended. They have been consecutively bumper-to-bumper. Dictatorships cannot thrive on peace. They need crises to justify their rule.

Anne O'Hare McCormick, writing for New York Times Magazine on May 7th, 1933, wrote approvingly of FDR's power grab:

> The American people, she observed, "trust the discretion of the President more than they trust Congress." Rather than a seizure of power of the kind that had brought the Bolsheviks or the Italian Fascists to power, the New Deal, she reported, rested on mass popular consent that "vests the president with the authority of a dictator. The authority is a free gift, a sort of unanimous power of attorney…all the other powers – industry, commerce, finance, labor, farmer and householder, State and city – virtually abdicate in his favor. America today literally asks for orders….Nobody is much disturbed by the idea of dictatorship." (p. 123)

Katznelson concludes his work in an Epilogue with a fearless, Pollyannish hope that America may continue on its Progressive path of statism to consolidate a "new national state," one founded by FDR and the New Deal. Have Americans consequently lost many of their liberties? Yes, answers Katznelson. But, *C'est la vie.*

But, *is* it life? No. Americans should realize that dictatorships and statism are, at core, profoundly *anti-life*. They ought to be fearful of and disturbed by a government that regularly, daily, as a matter of policy, robs them of the sovereignty of their own lives.

* *Fear Itself: The New Deal and the Origins of Our Time,* by Ira Katznelson. New York: Liveright/W.W. Norton, 2014. 720 pp.

April 2014

Magazine Review: A Moss-Covered Rolling Stone

Suppose someone buttonholed you on the street, a fellow wearing an aluminum pyramid for a hat, a blue jumpsuit with numerous pockets even on the pants legs, and L.L. Bean hiking boots, and who had intense, glazed-over eyes that sent a zing of fear up your spine but which invited you to enter his realm of demons and jins and unicorns. He begins spouting that the world is flat, that the moon is just a big mottled silver disk in the sky which if you stare at out of focus long enough you'd see the face of God smiling down at you, and that the stars were but pinholes filtering through the light of an alternate universe.

You know this fellow is more than a crackpot and that not much of the real universe is filtering through to his mind. You might listen to him for a while, more from pity than from anything else. You would throw glances around at passersby, wanting to communicate in embarrassment that you're not really with this fellow, but you don't want to tell him to buzz off, and please let go of the lapel of your jacket, because he just might have a gun or a knife in one of those pockets and not granola bars and packets of Trail Mix on which he seems to have been subsisting. You listen to him with effort, with a patient courtesy that is costing you sweat and physical strength because you're also restraining a desire to laugh in his face.

To make the experience endurable, you imagine you're Cary Grant, tied to a chair in the movie *Arsenic and Old Lace*, and that your seemingly lucid captor is Raymond Massey, an escaped lunatic from a mental asylum for the criminally insane who's claiming he's a master murderer....

That's how I felt when a friend recently forwarded to me an article from Rolling Stone, dated January 3rd, 2014, by Jesse A. Myerson. The headline itself made me blink in disbelief: "Five Economic Reforms Millennials Should Be Fighting For: Guaranteed jobs, universal basic incomes, public finance and more." Haven't these ideas been repudiated and discredited? I don't voluntarily read the Rolling Stone or the Village Voice or any other publication that seems to be published by aging hippies still celebrating Woodstock and the Weathermen. Myerson's article was news to me. I learned that it had been the subject of numerous clucking tongued critiques by fellow travelers and episodes of raspberries and roiling laughter from Left and Right alike. I was a newcomer to the piece. Better late than never.

The name, Jesse A. Myerson, meant nothing to me, until I searched for his name on the Internet and discovered that he was one of the "geniuses" – a "media coordinator" – behind Occupy Wall Street, that Marxist movement which drew tens of thousands to American cities several years ago. It petered out when reality intervened and the "occupiers," out of a sense of self-preservation, drifted back to warm homes and sanitary conditions and possibly even gainful employment. Doubtless some major publisher will concoct a book deal for Jesse Myerson. I wrote several columns about OWS, and won't reprise their conclusions here.

For example, Sean Davis at the Federalist wrote:

> But what makes Myerson's article so precious is that either he's too dumb to know what the Soviet Union stood for (or too lazy to have done a quick Google search prior to clicking "Publish"), or he thinks his readers are too dumb to discern that he's actually pushing for a return to Soviet-style communism. In his defense, he published his Marxist mash note at Rolling Stone — a site run by a seemingly drug-addled 23-year-old nepot — so maybe he has a point about the collective IQ of his readers.

"Dumb" is the operative term, together with cognitively-challenged and delusional. It is measurably easier to critique Myerson than it is to freeze-frame and examine every non sequitur of the mental gymnastics of someone like Nobelist in economics Paul Krugman.

Noel Sheppard at News Busters had some fairly simple questions to ask Myerson:

2. Social Security for All

> *But let's think even bigger. Because as much as unemployment blows, so do jobs. What if people didn't have to work to survive? Enter the jaw-droppingly simple idea of a universal basic income, in which the government would just add a sum sufficient for subsistence to everyone's bank account every month...A universal basic income, combined with a job guarantee and other social programs, could make*

participation in the labor force truly voluntary, thereby enabling people to get a life.

So why would we need to guarantee everyone a job with a good wage if folks didn't have to work as a result of a universal basic income?

And if people didn't have to work, who would produce the goods and services necessary for life on this planet?

And if no goods and services were being produced, where would the money come from to fund this universal basic income?

At the risk of offending *Star Trek* fans, Myerson writes as though he were cadging the elements of the communist society whose identity trickled through in the series, especially in the "Next Generation" seasons and as articulated by Captain Jean-Luc Picard of the Enterprise. He once told a survivor from the 20th century to "improve himself." This was after the character realizes that his capitalist fortune is no more and that he would not be permitted to amass another. Apparently, the government provides everyone with "room and board" and a chance to become a "useful" member of society – "voluntarily." Things like restaurants and vineyards and quilt tatting are mere personal "hobbies." Someone at the Science Fiction and Fantasy site had the sense to observe:

A big clue into their form of government is that fact that they have no monetary policy. They have no money [except "Federation credits"], which means they have no taxes, no expenditures, and no GDP. That raises the question, how do they finance their government? Regardless of what form that government takes, it needs resources to maintain itself.

Given the peace-oriented nature of the Federation, one would assume that those resources are given to the government voluntarily, including human resources in the form of political leadership. People volunteer their leadership in order to be accepted, rejected, or passively allowed, all in a non-forceful manner.

That's going to where no economist has gone before, except perhaps Paul Krugman.

To distance himself from those old fuddy-duddies Marx, Engels, and Proudhon (all property is theft, you know) – whose works he has likely never read from cover to cover – Myerson tries to sound hip and "with it" by writing in a grungy, sophomoric style and by pretending he's advancing a radically new political/economic system without once mentioning Communism, Stalin, and tyranny. He uses the slang term "blow" five times in the article. This blows, that blows, everything "blows." But obviously, no typhoons howl through Myerson's mind. For example, in his prefatory paragraphs, Myerson proclaims:

> Millennials have been especially hard-hit by the downturn, which is probably why so many people in this generation (like myself) regard capitalism with a *level of suspicion* that would have been *unthinkable* a decade ago. (*Italics* mine)

Myerson seems oblivious to the fact that previous generations of young people have maintained high, vociferous levels of "suspicion" against capitalism, not just his own. He might have overlooked the fact that a previous generation now owns the corridors of political power, and is attempting to ram their own "five" reforms down the country's throat (David Axelrod, Bill Ayers, *et al.*). And they were all on the same "thinkable" page. *Suspicion?* Say, rather, *hostility.*

Under his "Guaranteed Work for Everybody" subtopic, Myerson writes:

> There are millions of people who want to work, and there's a ton of work that needs doing – it's a no-brainer. And this idea isn't as radical as it might sound: It's similar to what the federal Works Progress Administration made possible during Roosevelt's New Deal...

Myerson gives Roosevelt a pat on the back. I think that's as far back in time he can go. But how long would it take one to persuade him that programs like the WPA helped to delay the country's recovery from a government-caused Depression, because all the money being redirected to it and other grandiose programs was confiscated private wealth that could have helped correct government-caused economic dislocations. But, perhaps because Myerson's grasp of causo-connections is so tenuous – in point of fact, virtually *imaginary* – the learning exercise would likely be futile. How many Flat Earthers are impervious to ample evidence that the world is round?

Under the same subtopic, Myerson assured us that:

> A job guarantee that paid a living wage would anchor prices, drive up conditions for workers at megacorporations like Walmart and McDonald's, and target employment for the poor and long-term unemployed – people to whom conventional stimulus money rarely trickles all the way down. The program would automatically expand during private-sector downturns and contract during private-sector upswings, balancing out the business cycle and sending people from job to job, rather than job to unemployment, when times got tough.

Try to make the pinball machine connections between "living wages," "anchored prices," and escalating worker conditions at Walmart and McDonald's. Myerson may as well have written: Apples plus Oranges Multiplied by Bananas Equals Cumquats. Notice how he stresses that his program would "expand during private-sector downturns" but "contract during private-sector upswings." Is he confessing that he would allow any private sector to exist?

News flash to Myerson: If actually implemented, his program would automatically absorb a "down-turned" private sector, guaranteeing that there would never be an "upswing" in it ever again. Observe the progress of Venezuela toward poverty under an aggressive socialist régime that is absorbing private sectors by the dozen. The only "upswinging" entity in that country is the government's fist.

And, besides, how could such a perfect socio-economic paradise, one which incorporated all five programs plus ones Myerson hasn't even imagined, generate or even experience "tough times"? Isn't such a program designed to prevent "tough times"? Isn't a "pure" communist economy supposed to be immune to business cycles, because ideally, there would *be* no businesses to cycle?

The silence is deafening, except for the gunshots and screams one might hear in Venezuela and other places undergoing a descent into destruction.

To elaborate on Noel Sheppard's News Busters critique, under "Social Security for All," Myerson poses the question:

> What if people didn't have to work to survive? Enter the jaw-droppingly simple idea of a **universal basic income**, in which the government would just add a sum sufficient for subsistence to everyone's bank account every month. (**Bolding** Myerson's)

Then some synapses must have crackled in his mind. If no one needed to work, who or what would produce the things an idle population could purchase with that "free" money? And where would that money come from, because if no one was producing anything, and if the means of production had been expropriated from the producers, there would be no tax revenue, either, to deposit in all those bank accounts. The government would need to tax itself. No, wait, that wouldn't work. It wouldn't happen, either. What would happen to Duke University Professor Kathi Weeks's idea of creating "time to cultivate new needs for pleasures, activities, senses, passions, affects, and socialities that exceed the options of working and saving, producing and accumulating"?

The synapses crackled faintly once more, and died.

> Put another way: A universal basic income, combined with **a job guarantee** and other **social programs**, could make participation in the labor force truly voluntary, thereby enabling people to **get a life**. (**Bolding** Myerson's)

And if you don't "volunteer" to participate, the government will seize your bank account, send you to a rehab camp in Death Valley where you can get your mind right, and subject you to a lobotomy to remove the last shred of independence you might have had.

In conclusion, Jesse Myerson subscribes to an ideology which, over many decades, has been oft refuted by thinkers like Thomas Sowell (Marxism: Philosophy and Economics), has been repudiated by individuals who endured and survived its depredations, and has demonstrated its intrinsic destructiveness wherever it has been tried. It is truly astonishing – to me, at least – that the ideology still has the power to fasten itself to anyone's mind and maintain an unshakable grip.

But, I shouldn't be so astonished, because without the unarticulated wish for the unearned and an effortless existence, the ideology would have no appeal and no chance of becoming encrusted in anyone's mind – encrusted, undigested, and deadening.

Myerson – together with the publication that was clueless or careless enough to publish his juvenile screed – is a rolling stone that does indeed gather the musty dead moss of Marxism.

March 2014

The Black Stone: Some Notes

I have no skill or aptitude for card games. A child could beat me at poker. I'm not good at second-guessing. I can't remember dealt cards, and have trouble remembering which combination of cards beats another.

But, if I knew nothing about a particular card game, and had to develop a scene in a novel that depended on how the game was played and who would win it, I would immerse myself in a study of the game and its milieu until I had dreams about it. Finished with the novel, I would retain some knowledge of the game but never concern myself with it again. The dreams would stop.

One of the personal delights of reading Ian Fleming's James Bond novels is a pure fascination with how Bond could take over a card or roulette game, or could make crucial observations about the way an enemy played golf. My favorite Bond coup occurs in <u>*Moonraker*</u>, in which he not only detects how a villain is cheating at <u>contract bridge</u>, but devises a way to foil the man and cause him to leave the exclusive men's club in London in a hurried and angry huff. And it is one of the few novels in which Bond doesn't get the girl at the end. That was Fleming's dark sense of humor at work.

Cyrus Skeen, the detective hero in *The Black Stone*, the sixth title in the series, finds himself in a similar situation. He knows little about Islam, and only a little more about Judaism. He is an atheist; a man's religion doesn't concern him, only his rationality (or lack of it). He is the wealthy son of lapsed Presbyterians. At one point in the story, he remarks to a character, "I can mock Judaism as well as the next religion, but not to a Jew's face." Or to any man's face, regardless of his religion. He demonstrates this rule in previous titles in the series. Religion is as far from his premier concerns as is contract bridge. And that naturally reflects on the author's concerns, as well.

In 1930, the time period in which the story is set, Islam was an alien creed few Americans had heard of. It was not regularly thrust into their consciousnesses as it is today. Nor was Judaism. But it is Islam, and not Judaism, that poses a peril in the story, just as it does today. Judaism is a religion; its adherents are not out to conquer or destroy the world. Islam, however, is more a political doctrine than it is a religion, and its inherent nature commands its proponents to seek global submission to it as the sole alternative to death. I have written extensively on this subject in the past, and won't repeat any of my arguments here.

Skeen is advised to familiarize himself with Islam. He undertakes that task. By novel's end, he has not reached the same conclusions about it as I have; he does not yet see that it is essentially political. What he does note is its savagery, particularly where Jews are concerned. Later, he realizes that the savagery can also be visited on non-Jews. Today, we know that no one is exempt from the *jihadi* agenda, not even dissenting Muslims. Skeen has only a mere handful of victims of that savagery to observe. We have millions.

In _The Black Stone_, Islam, its iconic and probably mythical prophet, its core texts, and its practices, are liberally mocked. This would come naturally to men in Skeen's time. Political correctness in thought and in speech did not exist. Fear of offending Muslims was a mindset reserved for our own time. The creed is too ludicrous for anyone to take seriously. Skeen doesn't even bother trying to imagine what Mohammad looked like. He just assumes that Mohammad was the Billy the Kid or the Clyde and Bonnie Barrow of his day, a brigand and a thief and a killer spreading "the word" by force, intimidation, and death.

One issue I do raise in the novel, but not to distraction, is the role of Western governments and Western oil companies in enabling Islam to become the threat it poses today. Oil companies were fairly certain that vast oil reserves lay beneath the blood-soaked sands of Arabia (not yet wholly Saudi) and in Persia, now Iran. Western governments, chiefly British and French, after World War I, carved up the former Ottoman Empire into utterly arbitrary Mandates which were later granted the status of sovereign states.

170.

Oil companies sought the aid of Western governments to interpose themselves on behalf of those companies in negotiations over exploration and drilling concessions with tribal leaders who were more successful in conquering and/or massacring their rivals. This is essentially the history of the Saudi dynasty that we know today, a family of squatters that thrives on stolen private property. Persia had a different background and a different history. Under President Herbert Hoover, the U.S. recognized Saudi Arabia on May 1st, 1931.

So, I do not focus exclusively on the fatal pragmatism of Western governments and oil companies, but raise the issue as a tantalizing clue to our current dilemma. Skeen's solution to dealing with nomadic barbarians, had he been faced with the question, would have been to recommend that the companies drill, drill, drill, and if attacked by Ibn Saud or Hussein Ali, or any other Arab mobster's tribe, to call in the Marines. And probably to plant the America flag on the whole sorry region, as we have on the Moon.

At the end of *The Chameleon*, in which Skeen has discovered and foiled a Nazi Bund, Skeen tells his wife that "Something wicked this way comes." In *The Black Stone*, he runs head on into a wickedness he could never have before imagined.

February 2014

HOLLYWOOD

The Death of Adult Movies

I rarely frequent movie theaters these days. Box office ticket prices are not the chief deterrent, nor the concession stand price of a barrel of popcorn or a box of Raisinets. Talkative members of audiences, and eardrum-splitting volumes of trailers are also deterrents, but they're not why I avoid ticket windows. Rather it's what's showing in the theaters that stops me from sitting in the dark. I will make an exception, and pay for a ticket, if I think I ought to see a film. If I make the effort, it's because I suspect there's something odd about a film that I wouldn't be able to identify unless I saw it instead of being misled or repelled by its trailers.

I happen to love movies. Good movies. Ones that uplift me, or instruct me in the art of storytelling, or enlighten me in some respect. But bad movies, or mediocre ones, have the same effect on me as does Andy Warhol's poster of Campbell Soup cans. And there are far more of those films than there are of that anti-artist's thirty-two soup cans.

I recently saw *The Hunger Games: Catching Fire*. I suspected that, like its predecessor, it was more than just a story about a girl good with a bow and arrow, coming from a circa 1930's West Virginia-like coal town, and populated with characters whose names seem to have been the result of a Scrabble game with no rules. The setting wasn't supposed to be a post-war or post-anarchy America governed by PanAm – excuse me, "Panem" – an oppressive government located in some high-tech run Imperial Rome-like city that's full of evil men and a populace of perversely effete, gaudily dressed clowns entertained by a form of gladiatorial combat. The weird names -- Katniss Everdeen, Peeta Mellark, Finnick Odair, etc., all vaguely Celtic – didn't fool me one bit, either. It was all an allegory on America.

So I learned that both *Hunger Games* movies – I saw the first one, also, and there will be a third, to judge by the ending of Number Two – were political statements about the evils of technology and capitalism and civilization and how virtuous living the simple life at a subsistence level trumps technology and cities and badly dressed people every time. The "message" was as thoroughly embedded in it as it was in another fantasy, *Avatar*.

As the American consciousness has been progressively foreshortened, minimalized, and cramped over several generations – chiefly by a public education philosophy committed not so much to the acquisition of knowledge and the honing of one's cognitive powers and rationality, as to what the Progressives and the government wish to have Americans focus on (anti-intellectualism, pragmatism, conformity) – so has the "I.Q." of films diminished in terms of scope, scale and attention span. This has occurred, not overnight, but incrementally, in generational jerks and spasms, in syncopated tandem with the dumbing down and the engineered cognitive and cultural myopia.

Instead of adapting novels that require a modicum of literacy and an extended attention span to read and grasp – an attention span beyond what a text message or a tweet demands – we are getting movies more and more adapted from graphic novels. From comic books. And if not from comic books, then from juvenile or "young adult" novels, or computer games. And often a computer-game-inspired movie will loop back into an advanced version of the game.

Left behind in this scramble for boffo box office receipts and securing the twenty-something and "tween" crowds are adults and adult themes and subjects (and I don't mean pornography). "Adult" themes and stories are about individual heroism, or integrity, or mature but rational relationships and conflicts, and even political issues and crime stories based on a rational ethics.

Instead of something like *Seven Days in May*, we get *Olympus has Fallen*. There are no razzmatazz special effects in the former, nor any Korean terrorists (nor any Islamic terrorists, for that matter, that wouldn't be

Sharia-Compliant; see my column on that subject here), just nonpareil direction, acting, and suspense, even though Burt Lancaster, as the coup-plotting general was intended to be the incarnation of the "right wing." It's the well-made films with the subtle, unemphasized "messages" that are the effective and memorable films, as well as the ones with no ostensive political or "social justice" messages at all, such as the original *The Browning Version*, *Leave Her to Heaven*, or *Laura*.

Want a gripping story of tragedy or personal conflict from an adult perspective? Try *Tunes of Glory*, *Tea and Sympathy*, or *The Runner Stumbles*. Want a good comedy? Try *Hobson's Choice*, *His Girl Friday*, *The Ladykillers*, or *Nothing Sacred*. Want a "romantic" movie that features "adult" conflicts without showing an inch of flesh? Try *Separate Tables*, *For Whom the Bell Tolls*, or *Brief Encounter*.

Either you will not find their counterparts in modern movies, or if they've been remade, they just don't evoke short-term memory, never mind nostalgia. The remakes especially are guilty of pointlessly changing names and situations to appeal to the current generation or the current political mantra. Too often those changes just don't make the grade. You wonder why producers and directors bother with a remake, until you see what they've done to the characters, the story, and the theme.

Needless to say, I won't be seeing *Captain America: The Winter Soldier*, just as I have refrained from seeing any of the *Dark Knight Trilogy*, or any of the other comic book-based action movies. I'm a full-grown adult. I don't need to be "entertained" by having my mind seared, scoured, and dulled by endless car chases, exploding CGI space ships, incredible fight scenes that induce mental whiplash, decibel-destroying automatic weapons, and flat acting. There should come a point in anyone's life when he should know that he's being patronized and insulted at the same time, but the capacity to make that connection is missing in more and more adults. "We're going to treat you like an adolescent, insult your intelligence, and take your money, too." No, thanks.

Someone might ask: But aren't these comic book movies upholding heroes and justice, things you are for? I don't know that this is true. When you project heroes and justice outside the realms of reality, that might be fine for children and adolescents exploring the value of heroism or moral issues for the first time, but it hardly applies to adults. Children, adolescents and adults might get a glimmering of how to solve a serious moral problem by watching *Executive Suite*, not *Wall Street*. Or *Shane*, not *The Wild Bunch*.

About a million words have already been written by reviewers and critics about *Captain America*, but few, to my knowledge (and I've read a hefty number of them), observe the adolescence-orientation of that film and its ilk, or they reveal that their authors are oblivious or indifferent to the phenomenon. Mike Wilmington of Movie City News, however, wrote an ambivalent column about the pros and cons of *Captain America: The Winter Soldier*, while still pining for something a little more substantial than the facile razzle-dazzle of modern action thrillers or adventure films. He opens with:

> In the mood for something super-duper, movie-wise? Something loud, fast, full of crash-bang and zip-zowie, and liable to make megazillions of dollars all around the world? **Captain America: The Winter Soldier** — which is the latest Marvel Comics super-hero spectacular — may be just your super-ticket.

> I'm being facetious, but maybe not super-facetious. The movie, directed by Anthony and Joe Russo, has a lot going for it, though I think it's being somewhat overrated. A super-hero picture with a great two-faced super-villain, a super-jittery action camera, super-CGI tricks, super-credit teasers, a shrewdly super-paranoid script, and a sort of a heart, Captain America: The Winter Soldier definitely belongs in the upper echelon of Marveldom, somewhere under **Iron Man** and **Spider-Man 2**, and somewhere above **The Hulk** and **X-Men**.

Discussing the plot of *Captain America*, Wilmington notes:

> These nightmare fantasies of the teen-targeted super-hero action movies (or SHAMS) and young adult movies (or YAMs) — so wildly popular with younger audiences — are fashioned out of the Marvel comic books of the '60s and '70s, which is when Marvel Comics main-man writer-editor **Stan Lee** wrote a lot of his best stuff and when I read a lot of it), and this Captain America (created for the comics by **Joe Simon** and **Jack Kirby**) is a *left-wing movie* that makes its

villains part of the military-industrial complex: self-righteous militarists who want to take over the world, and programmed mercenaries like the Winter Soldier himself. [*Italics* mine]

That observation can also be applied to the differences between the original *The Manchurian Candidate* (1962) and the remake (2004). The first was about a Communist conspiracy to install a president friendly to Communism. The second was about a capitalist plot to install a president friendly to capitalism. Some pundits have called President Barack Obama a "Manchurian Candidate." However, I'd call him the Ayers/Soros/Alinsky candidate. I might also add that when it comes to portraying a conspiring, manipulative mother-bear bitch, Meryl Streep can't hold a candle to Angela Lansbury.

Wilmington asks:

> Is it a bad joke that this truly super art form is now often most expensively used to make ultra-costly versions of old comic books (even good old comic books) and new young adult novels (even good ones), intended for a world-wide audience of teenagers, and people who seem to want to be teenagers? Are we so steeped in teen fantasies… that the real world and all the magnificent stories you can cull from it are relegated mostly to the smaller budgets and cheaper seats?

No, it isn't a bad joke. Something unfunny is at work. What is responsible for the "reimagining" of older material is moral and esthetic bankruptcy, with directors, producers, and most Hollywood studios suffering from selective autism, with a strong strain of Alinskyite target-and-destroyism.

Wilmington's plaintive remarks echo the subject of Diana West's seminal critique of American culture, *The Death of the Grownup: How America's Arrested Development is Bringing Down Western Civilization* (reviewed here).

In my column, "Maturity Deferred: The Death of the Grown-up," I wrote:

> West's central thesis is that our culture has ossified into a "perpetual adolescence," even though the Baby Boomer generation is nearing or at the age of retirement. That

generation was sired and raised by the "greatest generation," one of adults and even adolescents who fought World War Two in combat overseas and in the factories at home.

The "greatest generation," however, in turn raised a not-so-great generation many of whose members became the creators and proponents of or adherents to the rebellious "counterculture" of the 1960's and 1970's, with its pronounced leftist, collectivist and nihilist means and ends. If members of that generation did not actively take part in the assault on the status quo, then they passively accepted a besieged status quo as mere powerless spectators.

West diagnoses part of the problem, as I note in my column:

Throughout her book West cites numerous instances of adults abdicating or never discovering their responsibilities as thinking, reasoning adults. She defines two species of this state of purported adult "adolescence," a condition she also claims is exacerbated by multiculturalism and diversity:

A reluctance to assert or champion "adult" values one knows are superior, or a fear to assert them, lest one be accused of something terrible (fascism, elitism, or racism) by the enemies of those values;

An indoctrinated ignorance of or hostility to any values that are demonstrably superior.

Lest anyone accuse me of retreating to the past, let him. Today's culture and arts are not mine. I am not so much alienated from the culture, as it is alien to everything I hold dear. And I think that anyone who has read this column up to this point would agree that they're grown-ups, too.

April 2014

Lawrence of Arabia: A Reappraisal

When you move through the years and acquire knowledge of things you liked and the wisdom to dislike them when they show their true colors, it is time to put some distance between you and the objects of that youthful admiration.

For me, at least, this is true of that great 1962 epic, "Lawrence of Arabia." I first saw it in my senior year of high school, in 1963. It knocked me flat, psychologically speaking. I had a free pass to the movie theater in which it was showing; I must have seen it a dozen times. Today, in retrospect, I cannot say anything against the direction, cinematography, cast, Robert Bolt's screenplay, and grand scale theme of the picture. They all met the criteria of what a movie should meet when a director intends it to be a defining epic. I did not care much for director David Lean's later pictures. Yet, "Lawrence of Arabia" in no small way influenced my desire to become a novelist.

The occasion of actor Peter O'Toole's death on December 14th apparently prompted Israeli writer and TV commentator Reuven Berko to pen a column "The Final Death of Lawrence of Arabia." O'Toole made a spectacular screen debut playing T.E. Lawrence. It won several Oscars, a Golden Globe, a BAFTA, and was even nominated for a Saturn Award by the Academy of Science Fiction, and Horror Films. In his article, Berko does what I had wanted to do for years, but had other writing commitments to meet: call director David Lean's bluff.

Berko begins appropriately enough:

> Peter O'Toole, who was marvelous in "Lawrence of Arabia," died recently. Many commentators and critics feel that Lawrence's story and the movie about him influenced the actions of many European statesmen, politicians, and members of Western foreign ministries and security services. However, there is considerable argument as to whether and what, as a matter of historical fact, T. E. Lawrence contributed to the British war effort by collaborating with the Bedouin tribes of the Arabian Peninsula against the Ottoman Turks during the First World War. Not all historians agree to

the truth of the glowing reports of his personality, moral stature and personal behavior.

Ever since "Lawrence" debuted in theaters so long ago, it has become political and cultural policy not to speak ill of either T.E. Lawrence or the Arabs. David Lean's stock of knowledge about the Middle East and Islam is, at this point, unknown, and is hardly the issue. However, it could be said that he pioneered and popularized the politically correct way of viewing and portraying Islam and Lawrence himself. Berko writes:

> Nevertheless, the enigmatic figure of Lawrence, an intelligence officer, became a role model for Western diplomats and statesmen, and he is revered as a master of mediating with the leaders of the Arab world. He seemed secretive and manipulative, with the rare ability and knowledge to exploit Arab ideology to achieve victory and foster the interests of the West, and to build inter-cultural cooperation and coexistence in a way that was both noble and romantic.

> The Arabs with whom Lawrence collaborated were romanticized and made to appear exotic and other-worldly. The murder, grudges, blood feuds, treachery, deception, destruction, violence, theft, robbery and looting, all deeply ingrained in the psyches of the Arab tribes, were wrapped in romanticism and existentialist concepts explained and justified as necessary, forced upon the Bedouins by their daily struggle to subsist in the hard conditions imposed on them by the desert.

> That was the foundation for utterly false and baseless concepts such as "Arab honor" and "his word is his bond," from which the image of the noble, almost feral, desert Bedouin Arab was constructed.

Over time, ever since first seeing "Lawrence," I grew to distrust any epic based on the life of an actual historic person. After all, to make a story interesting, the writer must put words into such a person's mouth he never spoke, and have him take actions he never took. Few are the movies in which the historic person is accurately depicted in word and deed, and they are, as a rule, as dull as dishwater. The more I learned about Arabs,

Islam, and the Middle East over the years, the more I questioned the value of "Lawrence," not as an esthetic or literary value, but as a vessel of truth.

Many years ago I owned a facsimile of Lawrence's opus, *The Seven Pillars of Wisdom*, an autobiographical account of his role in the "Great Arab Revolt." As an adventure story purportedly based on fact, it has few parallels. But even as I read it then, questions occurred to me about the overall veracity of the tale. There are virtually no critical statements in the book about the Arabs or Islam. Berko notes:

> Few people have bothered to read the *Muqaddimah*, or *Introduction,* written by Arab historian Ibn Khaldun in the 14th century, in which he describes the Bedouins as destructive, lacking any sense of morality or values, and working only to destroy culture and world order. Even fewer have read Fouad Ajami's 1998 book, *The Dream Palace of the Arabs: A Generation's Odyssey*, with its painful criticism of the pitiful Arab, whose inherent culture left him no shred of sincerity, creativity or courage. Worse, even fewer members of Arab society itself have dared to honestly criticize its faults for fear of reprisals.

What is the nature of that fear? The knowledge of the fact that Islam is a vindictive ideology, murderously jealous of its myths and fabrications and falsity.

> Peter O'Toole was a great actor, but the movie "Lawrence of Arabia" was nothing more than a Hollywood fantasy which, like the imaginary story of Lawrence, swept away many romantics and for decades had a negative impact on the decisions made by influential Western officials and statesmen dealing with policy in the Middle East. The problem is that today as well, Western leaders and policy-makers view and discuss the problems of the Middle East through the prism of Lawrence of Arabia, romantic, distorted and nostalgic as it is, seeing only the unilateral Arab position of every conflict, and adopting paradigms, symbols and historical deceptions as the gospel truth.

Islam has a reputation it cannot live down, which is that it is responsible for an enormous portion of human misery in history. From its very beginnings in the 7th century up through the Crusades, covering the raids of Moslem raiders for slaves on Europe as far north as Iceland, its built-in denigration and persecution of Jews, up to our own sorry times, Islam, and the Arabs, have a rap sheet engrossed with little else but blood, destruction, and death. However, as Berko writes:

> Lies told repeatedly, as the past has shown, become historical truths. Actually, Hollywood's world of dreams and fantasy did not penetrate the wandering sand dunes of the evil and unjust acts perpetrated by the Arabs and Bedouins throughout the years of the *jahiliyya* (the era of ignorance before Islam) which left their indelible imprint of murder and theft. Those crimes accompanied the Arabs and Muslims from the rise of Islam and accompany them to this day. All the evil storms of history visited upon humanity did not expose to the people of Europe (who today host well-established enclaves of radical Islam in their midst) even the surface of the slaughter and injustice carried out by Muslims in the name of Islam, "the religion of peace," against Jews and Christians.

About "Lawrence of Arabia" itself, I have a number of criticisms.

Inaccuracies abound in the film. For example, the still which illustrates Berko's IPT article is taken from the scene when Lawrence is in one of his "emotional" states, pulled in one direction to lead his army on to Damascus and triumph and bypass a retreating Turkish column, and in another to attack the column, partly in vengeance for the gruesomely slaughtered Arab village of Tafas the Turks have left behind, and partly for his rape by the Turks in Daraa. The column is massacred, but there is no scene depicting an attached German army unit that successfully fought off the attacking tribesmen.

Also, in that scene is briefly shown a Saudi warrior or prince with the green Saudi banner. However, the Saudis, who at the time were just another tribe vying for prominence, were not allies of Lawrence, who was fighting for the rival Hashemites and Hussein, the Sharif and Emir of Mecca. So, that warrior just didn't belong there. The Saudis later conquered all of the Arabian peninsula without Lawrence's help (but with plenty of British help; by then, Lawrence, ever flighty, had retired and gone into hiding in the Army and the RAF as a mechanic under the names

181.

of Shaw and Ross), dispossessing Hussein of his titles. He retired to Amman, in what is now Jordan.

Another gross inaccuracy was the attack on Aqaba. A daring charge is depicted in the movie, but in fact the Turks had agreed to a surrender of the town and Lawrence's Arab army simply walked in. There are photographs of the "charge." I could go on with more inaccuracies and inconsistencies, but I think I've made my point.

I must agree with Berko; the movie does romanticize the Arabs, and inflates Lawrence's role in the Arabs' fight for "independence." But this romanticization of Arabs and Islam is nothing new; writers and artists have been doing that for nigh on two centuries. See Ibn Warraq's excellent book, *Sir Walter Scott: The Crusades and Other Fantasies*, for example (discussed in my column, "The Fraudulent Frankenstein of Islam" on Rule of Reason and other blog sites). Painting the Islamic Arabs in rosy colors doesn't do justice to them; they remain "greedy, barbarous, and cruel," in no small part because of the nature of Islam itself.

Another thing wrong with the picture is that it creates the false impression that the Arabs were all one big happy but occasionally dysfunctional family, exploited by Turks and British alike, ready to unite against the British colonialists but often descending into petty squabbling and bickering, some of it comical, some of it leading to bloodshed. In fact, the various Bedouin tribes at the time were constantly at each other's throats, raiding caravans and villages in interminable turf wars. Some of this is depicted in the film. One of the few honest lines of dialogue in the picture was spoken by Anthony Quinn as Auda Abu Tayi: "Arab? What tribe is that?"

Historically, tribal contentions, claims, and warfare can be exemplified by the rivalry between Hussein bin Ali, putative Sharif and Emir of Mecca, of the Hashemites, and the tribal Sauds, headed by Wahhabist Ibn Saud (Abdulaziz). Doctrinal differences in Islam contributed to their contest for power over not only the Arabian Peninsula, but "Arab" lands as far away as present day Yemen. The Sauds wanted to rule everything "Arab," but so did Hussein. T.E. Lawrence was sent by the British to advise the Hashemites; later, however, the British sided with the Sauds. In this reversal, British policy was aided by another one of those "desert-loving English," Hillary St. John Bridger Philby, an intelligence officer who originally sided with Hussein, but also persuaded the British to put their support behind the Sauds. Philby and Lawrence differed on which band of avaricious cutthroats deserved British support. Lawrence "went native" only as far as his dress and his sympathies. Philby converted to Islam. His son, Kim Philby, became a Soviet double agent.

David Lean's movie was partly inspired by playwright Terence Rattigan's stage play, "Ross," which in various productions has starred Alec Guinness, John Mills, Ian McKellen, and Simon Ward in the title role. Being a collector of Rattigan's works, I still have a copy of the Hamish Hamilton edition of the play with Guinness on the front cover that is featured in the linked Wikipedia article. Many of the key incidents that occur in the film were taken or adapted from Rattigan's play. Robert Bolt, the screenwriter, performed a superb job of "blowing up" the play to help produce an hours-long, sun-soaked cinematic epic. The most valuable lesson I have profited from in the screenplay was the importance of dialogue.

Today, we really haven't much to thank T.E. Lawrence for, unless it was his qualified and debatable contribution to the rise of Arab nationalism and the ossification and then growth of Islam as an ideological nemesis.

January 2014

Hollywood: Sharia-Compliant

Hollywood has rarely produced a trustworthy depiction of historical events. My own philosophy of historical fiction is that historic events should serve as background to the conflicts, aspirations, ambitions, betrayals and destiny of the principal characters in the story. Further, the plot in which these characters move – or, even better, when these characters move the plot itself – should not conflict with the historic events, but be in sync with those events. The principal conflicts should be between the characters, not between the story and history. I obeyed this rule while writing the *Sparrowhawk* series, and also my period detective novels.

Hollywood does not adhere to such rules. I don't think it has even formulated them.

Thus we have such examples as the 1936 *Charge of the Light Brigade*, in which the sequence of events of the Indian Mutiny and the Crimean War was reversed (the war, 1853-1856; the mutiny, 1857). Otherwise it would have required Errol Flynn to survive the Charge and travel to India to rescue Olivia de Havilland from Surat Khan's filthy clutches. History was tweaked, but not by much, to accommodate the plot. The lavish 1968 Tony Richardson version, however, was a plotless anti-war statement, complete with animated period political cartoons and caricatured Victorian figures. And, because it was an anti-war statement, it was gorier than its predecessor.

There are innumerable films and TV series grounded in history. I could write a book about the subject. I might do that, some day. What looms largest in my mind, however, and at the moment, is David Lean's *Lawrence of Arabia* (1962). At the age of 17, when I first saw it shortly after its release, I was literally smitten by it. It got me to read up on World War One. Although I entertained doubts about its accuracy, it was a grand scale film, one of the last. My positive appraisal of it gradually diminished over the years, the more I learned about how and why the Allied campaign in the Middle East was conducted.

Clinching my final negative appraisal was Efraim Karsh's August 9th, 2013 article, "Seven Pillars of Fiction," originally published in the Wall Street Journal and reprinted by the Middle East Forum. It concluded that

Lawrence was indeed a consummate charlatan, and that the "Arab Revolt" was a fiction invented by one ambitious Arab potentate and cashed in on by another, the Saudi "king," Abdul Aziz ibn Saud. Saud sat out the war and did not participate in any of the warfare conducted against the Turks by Lawrence under the aegis of Hussein ibn Ali, the putative "Sharif of Mecca," and Prince Faisal, one of his sons. Hussein also sought the title, "King of the Arabs." I provide many more details of this pragmatic episode of "nation building" in my detective novel, *The Black Stone*.

It also led me to the conclusion that David Lean, one of the finest film directors to ever peer through a camera lens, was just another ingenuous dupe of the legend of Lawrence of Arabia. At the time, questioning the stature of T.E. Lawrence would have been treated as slanderous heresy. His film, which I still maintain is a magnificent example of what films *could be*, was inspired by and produced as a result of the success of Terence Rattigan's 1960 play, *Ross*, which was closer to the truth in its depiction of Lawrence than was *Lawrence of Arabia*.

I've often written about Hollywood's Leftist, anti-American crusade, and its penchant for obliging the sensibilities of offended Muslims in the past, for example, here, here, here, here, and most recently, here, about the Disney/ABC Family Group's capitulation to the demands of the Hamas-connected Council of American-Islamic Relations (CAIR) that it cancel a TV program, "Alice in Arabia." Nick Provenzo wrote about the murder of Dutch filmmaker Theo Van Gogh in 2006, why Hollywood had little or nothing to say about it, and why Hollywood changed the villains from Muslims to "neo-fascists" in the production of Tom Clancy's novel, *The Sum of All Fears*. Wikepedia has the "low-down" on why the villains' identities were changed. The screenwriter, Dan Pyne, protesteth too much.

The Disney/ABC decision garnered little or no mention in the mainstream media, nor did the announcement that Disney/ABC would work with Muslim screenwriters to produce future programs that would not offend Muslim feelings or invite chares of blasphemy or "slandering" the good name of Islam. The Muslim Public Affairs Council (MPAC), a Muslim Brotherhood front group, announced also that it would provide Disney/ABC with this "talent."

That boils down to: MPAC wonks voluntarily installed by Disney/ABC as paid censors of its output. It means: Disney/ABC is willing to submit to

Islamic Sharia law, and avoid any criticism of Islam, and the Muslim wonks will be there to ensure that Disney/ABC complies.

(I have sent this column to the executives of Disney/ABC Family Group. It would be interesting to know that they have read the MPAC links provided in the foregoing paragraphs – that is, if they wish to bother to learn with whom they are partnering. As for the history of CAIR, that's pretty much public knowledge, and I'm sure those executives know the history, too.)

Have Hollywood studios no shame? Apparently not, if shame is regret for betraying one's freedom for some tenuous notion of "security." Hollywood has been submitting to all kinds of pressure for decades: to federal pressure, Communist pressure, union pressure, feminist pressure, "gay rights" pressure – and Islamic pressure. This is aside from the Hays Office of censors, which exercised its own moral arm-twisting on Hollywood back in the 1930's.

Islamic dhimmitude is just the latest chapter in Hollywood's submission to threats, regulations, and "social pressure" to produce what is acceptable film fare at the moment. While the Hays Office expired in the 1950's, and beginning in the 1960's the Production Code succumbed to the Left's film philosophy that anything goes and the only stricture is something called "parental guidance," Hollywood remains in thrall to whomever fills the vacuum of "moral uplift" and shakes a vigorous fist at Tinsel Town.

It's generally thought that it doesn't matter if Hollywood succumbs to self-censorship, to government regulation and censorship, or even to Islamic censorship because, as one reader of a Breitbart article on the tapping of Kevin Spacey to play Winston Churchill in a future production, remarked, "Rational people have the ability to realize it's just a fictional show and don't change their opinions on whom to vote for because of a TV show." (This was in reference to Spacey's hit TV series, "House of Cards.")

Here I expand on my reply to the reader's comments:

> Rational people don't denigrate, debunk, or satirize their political affiliations or their political principles. Nor do they wish to see them denigrated, debunked, or mocked – not unless they think it doesn't matter, that they'll come out on

top, and people don't take ideas seriously anyway, they're just a bunch of goofballs.

Kevin Spacey is basically a nihilist. He can dramatize the truth about how Washington works, and believes telling the truth won't matter. He thinks his Democratic Party will still triumph and continue to put the screws to the American people. He counts on people thinking: Well, it's only TV, it's only actors, and sets, and scripts, no one will take it seriously. It's just "entertainment."

However, fiction and film have a more powerful effect on people's minds and the course of politics than you might realize, especially if they're well done, as "House of Cards" was. If they didn't, no one would bother writing political fiction or making political films. Why did Oliver Stone make *JFK* or any of his other political films? To influence viewers. Why do leftists and conservatives blow a gasket when any of Ayn Rand's novels are mentioned? It's because they're afraid her novels will influence readers by showing the evil of statism and the consequences of selflessness. Why did Khomenei issue a death fatwa on Salman Rushdie and call for the banning of *The Satanic Verses*? Because he and his mullahs believed his book would damage Islam, so they called it "blasphemous." People do respond to political films, novels, and satire whether or not they realize they're just fiction, and their producers and directors know this.

This is why the executives behind Disney/ABC's cancellation of "Alice in Arabia" at the behest of terrorist front group, CAIR, don't think it matters. It's just a TV show, people won't take it seriously, and won't miss it if they never see it. And, besides, we really don't want to get the Saudis mad at us. Why, they could buy a controlling interest in Disney/ABC. That would be too much. We're willing to cooperate. And our female executives might not want to wear head scarves or Hefty trash bags. We don't want people thinking ill of the Saudis, or of Islam.

Not allowing TV audiences to see it, however, misses the point. It was a conscious decision to cancel the show. It's as significant an action – moral cowardice – as if a "Gang Busters" radio drama from the 1930's was cancelled on the complaint of Al Capone or Frank Nitti some other gangster, because the show allegedly "stereotyped" gangsters or gave people the "wrong idea" about the character of gangsters. But the truth about Islam is that it is brutal, primitive, and totalitarian in nature. Saudi Arabia is a theocratic monarchy determined to perpetuate itself and corrupt the West, in particular, America. King Abdullah is a grosser caricature, physically and metaphorically, of a gangster than was Al Capone. Forget Batman's nemeses, the Joker, the Riddler and the Penguin. King Abdullah can't be exaggerated.

What happened to the initial motive to produce a show that depicts the efforts of an American girl kidnapped by Saudis to escape her captors? It was regretted, suppressed, and discarded. Disney/ABC waved the white flag. Please don't accuse us of "Islamophobia"!

To date, Hollywood has not produced a single film or TV series in which the villains are Muslims or Muslim terrorists, not even *24*. It's usually "Serbian" nationalists, or South Africa-based neo-Nazis, or some other concocted terrorist group with designs on the U.S. But never Muslims. If Muslims appear on *24* or in some film, they're usually portrayed as blameless "innocents." Daniel Greenfield, in his January 24th column, "Hollywood's Muslim Lies," noted about *The Sum of All Fears*":

> Its writer Dan Pyne dismissed Islamic terrorism as a "cliché"; even though a plot can't be a cliché when it never appears in movies, only in real life. Pyne however found a more realistic villain. "I think, there was some neo-nationalist activity in Holland, and there was stuff going on in Spain and in Italy. So it seemed like a logical and lasting idea that would be universal."

Later, about cliché-burdened Pyne, Greenfield wrote;

> Instead Dan Pyne went on to write a remake of *The Manchurian Candidate* in which Communist China was replaced by the "Manchurian Corporation". He's currently working on a movie featuring a Syrian rescue worker who gets mistaken for a terrorist while trying to save lives during Hurricane Katrina. It's a cliché, but it's the kind of cliché that Hollywood likes.

If a movie is made about September 11 a decade from now, the villains will probably be Serbian nationalists. It would be a cliché to have 19 Muslim hijackers murder 3,000 people. And then the camera will linger meaningfully on a Muslim rescuer wrongly taken into custody by a bigoted NYPD cop who is overlooking the real Serbian/Dutch neo-nationalist corporate villains.

The original 1962 *Manchurian Candidate* is a taut, suspenseful, knuckle-chewing, unabashedly political film starring Frank Sinatra and Laurence Harvey. Its IMDB synopsis reads: "A former Korean War POW is brainwashed by Communists into becoming a political assassin." The 2004 "remake" stars Denzel Washington (an otherwise fine actor, but who possesses poor judgment about what kinds of films he appears in) in the Frank Sinatra role and is a convoluted, unabashedly politically correct, anti-business mess that blames, not a Communist plot to seize the White House, but a high-tech arms dealer, the "Manchurian Corporation." The purposeful butchery of the original story was called a "reimagining."

"Reimagine" the American Revolution as a French plot to install George Washington as "George the First" of America, or the Civil War as a British plot to dissolve the United States to perpetuate slavery. Or, "reimagine" American history as told by Howard Zinn and "Common Core." And how many times can anyone retell Custer's Last Stand, or "reimagine" *The Front Page*, *The Big Clock*, and *The Four Feathers* to fit the politically correct sensibility of the moment? I guess until there's as little connection between an original film and its latest "remake" as between a trumpet swan and a tomtit.

Finally, there's that old reliable government-business partnership to fall back on when looking for extra revenue and capitalization, otherwise known as fascism. Dreamworks went to China. The Los Angeles Times reported in February 2012:

> The creator of the "Shrek" movies said it was forming Oriental DreamWorks, a joint venture with China Media Capital and Shanghai Media Group in concert with Shanghai Alliance Investment – an investment arm of the Shanghai municipal government – to establish a family entertainment company in China.

189.

With an initial investment of $330 million, the Shanghai studio would develop original Chinese animated and live-action movies, TV shows and other entertainment catering to the China market. The deal was among several business ventures announced in downtown Los Angeles during an economic forum attended by visiting Chinese Vice President Xi Jinping, who is widely expected to be the country's next leader....

The new studio, which has been recruiting some staff in Hollywood, plans to begin operations later this year and could eventually surpass the size of DreamWorks' headquarters, which employs more than 2,000 people, Chief Executive Jeffrey Katzenberg said in an interview.

You can bet that Dreamworks China will not be producing animated films about the freedom of speech, the right of political protest, free enterprise, and individual rights. No, it will be producing more "Kung Fu Panda" films, and maybe a "reimagined" "Shrek" as Chairman Mao.

It had to be the natural course of moral collapse that Hollywood, dominated by the anti-American, anti-business, anti-esthetics, post-deconstructionist Left, would ally itself with anti-freedom, totalitarian Islam. It comports with the Muslim Brotherhood's agenda of sabotaging the West from within. The Brotherhood's May 22nd, 1991 memorandum details how especially America can be conquered and made Sharia complaint. The Investigative Project reported:

Written sometime in 1987 but not formally published until May 22, 1991, Akram's 18-page document listed the Brotherhood's 29 likeminded "organizations of our friends" that shared the common goal of dismantling American institutions and turning the U.S. into a Muslim nation. These "friends" were identified by Akram and the Brotherhood as groups that could help convince Muslims "that their work in America is a kind of grand Jihad in eliminating and destroying the Western civilization from within and 'sabotaging' its miserable house by their hands ... so that ... God's religion [Islam] is made victorious over all other religions."

190.

Thus the "grand jihad" [....] envisioned was not a violent one involving bombings and shootings, but rather a stealth (or "soft") jihad aiming to impose Islamic law (Sharia) over every region of the earth by incremental, non-confrontational means, such as working to "expand the observant Muslim base"; to "unif[y] and direc[t] Muslims' efforts"; and to "present Islam as a civilization alternative." At its heart, Akram's document details a plan to conquer and Islamize the United States – not as an ultimate objective, but merely as a stepping stone toward the larger goal of one day creating "the global Islamic state."

Hollywood is but one miserable wing of the "house" the Brotherhood and its Islamic terrorist allies wish to bring down and convert to their own brand of totalitarianism. Just as the Soviets infiltrated our government and our culture in the 1930's, including Hollywood, just as Hollywood obeyed Washington and refrained from producing movies during World War II critical of our totalitarian ally, Josef Stalin's Soviet Russia, Islam has made a key beachhead in Hollywood, to guide its Leftist denizens in the Sharia way.

Ultimately, it will not be the Brotherhood's hands that will help to destroy America, but the pragmatic, amoral, manicured hands of Hollywood, busy "reimagining" it.

March 2014

Hollywood's Selective "Islamophobia"

They are rankled! Upset! Angry! Outraged! Hair brushes could be made from their raised hackles! They're gnashing their teeth! Balling their fists, straining their massaged tendons, and cutting their palms with their manicured nails! They're really, really mad! It's unconscionable! We won't tolerate it! Their Gucci knickers are in such a twist they have a hard time picketing and not walking funny! We just won't come here anymore!!! *Take that*, Sultan of Brunei!

How dare the Sultan of Brunei, who owns some of our favorite party spots, want to stone to death gays, and lesbians, and even transgenderites, and people of all sixteen lifestyles who make whoopee outside marriage, or even if they're not married?? *Our* kinds of people!!!And isn't cutting off the hands of thieves just a bit *harsh*, damn it all? Over here, we let thieves off with a fine and a warning. And that rule about *no drinking*?? Criminey! Unacceptable! No gambling?? *That's* criminal!!!

The Clarion Project (which unfortunately is dedicated to "challenging 'extremism' and "promoting dialogue," much as many of the Hollywood protesters do), on May 7th reported:

> As Clarion Project previously reported, as of April 1, the first phase of *sharia* law went into effect in the country. Eventually, punishments including the stoning to death for the crimes of adultery, homosexuality and blasphemy and the amputation of limbs for theft will be implemented.

> Jay Leno, who participated in the protest organized outside the hotel, said, "I'd like to think that all people are basically good and that when they realize that this is going on, hopefully, they will do something about it ... I mean, it's just ... I don't know. Berlin, 1933? Hello, does it seem that far off from what happened during the Holocaust?"

> Other celebrities and business people are joining in the boycott, including comedians Stephen Fry and Ellen DeGeneres, and TV host Sharon Osbourne. British billionaire Richard Branson, owner of the Virgin Group, said in a tweet: "No @virgin employee, nor our family, will stay

at Dorchester Hotels until the Sultan abides by basic human rights."

Jay Leno, who at one point joined the protests, and speaking without cue cards and with no big adoring audience hanging on his every punch line, mumbled his incoherency about Berlin, and 1933, and the Holocaust. (He really shouldn't say anything in public without cue cards or a script.) But then his wife, Mavis, has been after the women-brutalizing Taliban in Afghanistan for a long time.

But women are brutalized by Sharia elsewhere in the world, as well, by Islam. Not just in Afghanistan. Try the Sudan, and Libya, and Yemen, and Saudi Arabia, and Iran, and Jordan, and Gaza, the West Bank, Pakistan, Nigeria, Indonesia, Malaysia, the Persian Gulf emirates. And in the Netherlands, Germany, France, Belgium, the U.K., Ireland, Scandinavia, Spain, Italy, all those former Soviet Central Asian republics whose names end with "stan." Austria. The U.S. and Canada. And Australia.

The Clarion Project pointed out this disparity between the outrage over Muslim Brunei and instances of other Islamic nations that have investments in the U.S.

> Christopher Cowdray, the chief executive of the London-based Dorchester Collection of hotels owned by Brunei, said it was unjust to single out the Beverly Hills Hotel and its employees. "There are other hotel companies in this city that are owned by Saudi Arabia ... you know, your shirt probably comes from a country which has human rights issues," said Cowdray.

> "This is misguided," Robert Anderson, the great-grandson of the founder of the hotel, told Reuters after the vote. "We should be against human rights violations in all countries, not just the Brunei."

However, the Sultan of Brunei's wanting to turn his country into an Islamic prison is nothing new. Islam has been practicing these things since long, long before Brunei was a gleam in the eyes of the Sultan's ancestors. Since the seventh century.

So, where were all these hair-tearing protesters forty years ago? Or when Islamic terrorists began hijacking airplanes? Why do some of these same protesters run Boycott Israel campaigns, and wish to see Israel torn from limb to limb? Why are they just now becoming "conscious" of Sharia? Have they the teeniest notion of how many hundreds of thousands of Muslims and non-Muslims have been meted the harshest Islamic "justice" over the centuries?

Perhaps not. While the mainstream media shies away from reporting honor killings, rapes, murders, domestic terrorism and related Islamic activities just in this country, the Internet is awash with news sites that do report these things. Hollywood types don't read these sites. Their "social justice" mentors advise them not to.

Where was their "Islamophobia" then? Or is it "Islamophobia"? I'm willing to bet that if one asked at random any of the outraged demonstrators against the Sultan if they were "Islamophobic," they'd scream bloody murder in denial. "What do you think I am? A racist?" Of course, a Malaysian or Brunei Muslim is not of the same "race" as a Pakistani or Arab or Turkish Muslim. Nor even of the same race as a chalk-white British convert to Islam. Still, the charge of "Islamophobia" is attended by the charge of "racism."

Of course, they don't condemn Islam. Islam is such a colorful religion, what with all that praying and prayer mats and pretty architecture and flowing garb. It's all so culturally diverse, you see. Sharia has nothing to do with Islam. Right? They can divorce Islam from Sharia and not be caught condemning Islam. CAIR will never file a slander suit against Jay Leno. Leno was smart. He didn't equate Sharia with Islam, either. Nor with jihad. Or perhaps he commits the same error, that is, segregates Sharia from Islam.

As for their favorite pre- and post-Oscar party palaces, and venues in which to spend lots and lots of money and network over drinks with their favorite people and pose with their latest squeezes for the pesky paparazzi, the Sultan gave them fair warning last October. Richard Ehrlich in his Washington Post article of October 22nd last year, "Brunei to implement Shariah penal code, including stoning, caning," reported:

> The sultan of Brunei announced on Tuesday (Oct. 22) he
> will rule his oil-rich Islamic country according to Shariah

laws, including death by stoning for adultery, the amputation of limbs for theft, flogging for alcohol consumption and abortion, and other punishments.

The Shariah penal code will begin in phases starting in April 2014, said Sultan Hassanal Bolkiah, according to Agence France-Presse.

John Walker, writing for Western Free Press on May 8th, in his article, "Hollywood Hypocrisy Cracks: Stars Boycott Historic Hotel Over Sharia Law," remarked:

> The stars spoke out when the Sultan of Brunei, who owns the hotel through a holding company, announced that his country would adopt Sharia law. The law is a brutal doctrine that calls for harsh treatment of violators of its legal and religious code – especially women and homosexuals.
>
> In a rare turnabout, Hollywood put aside its left-wing obsession with all things conservative – Christianity, the military, and free market capitalism. Hollywood wants the Sultan to divest the hotel from its holdings. But now it has opened a debate that goes far beyond one hotel on Sunset Boulevard.

The hypocrisy of Hollywood is obviously relevant here, but it's not my main point. Hollywood has always been hypocritical. Over the last four or so decades, it has churned out numerous anti-American, anti-military, pro "social justice" films, all the while enjoying the rule of law which they want to change in this country, and doing its own kind of wealth-spreading to countless tyros, producers, directors, actors, and actresses, turning them into millionaires or better, ready to tow the Progressive/Left party line.

It's the inbred, nearly incestuous cluelessness of the whole town. What Hollywood isn't quite aware of is the stake Islam has in their business (aside from the self-imposed injunction against negative portrayals of Islam and Muslims in films). Ben Shapiro, in his Breitbart column of May 7th, "Nine Other Sharia-financed Projects Hollywood Should Boycott," noted:

Brunei will now operate under laws that "call for violent punishment, including amputation and death by stoning, against those engaging in same-sex activity and extramarital sexual relations and those committing adultery." And as Big Hollywood's John Nolte stated:

"Hopefully, rather than using gay rights as a weak and hypocritical excuse to single out and beat up on conservative Christians, this is the first step of a Hollywood that will use its awesome power to call attention to the very real and tragic horrors homosexuals face in Islamic countries."

In honoring that "first step," we hereby recommend that Hollywood leverage its massive market power against other Sharia law targets.

The Movie *Promised Land.* Matt Damon's anti-fracking diatribe was funded by the royal family of the United Arab Emirates. As Lachlan Markey of Heritage Foundation writes, "*Promised Land* was also produced 'in association' with Image Media Abu Dhabi, a subsidiary of Abu Dhabi Media…The company is wholly owned by the government of the UAE."

The Abu Dhabi Film Festival and The Dubai Film Festival. Stars like Uma Thurman and Adrian Brody have attended the Abu Dhabi Film Festival. And the Dubai Film Festival – Dubai is a member of the UAE as well -- has attracted celebrities including Cate Blanchett, Tom Cruise, George Clooney, Oliver Stone, Gerard Butler, Salma Hayek, Richard Gere, Ben Affleck, Brad Bird, and others.

Al Jazeera America. Al Gore had no problem taking hundreds of millions of dollars from the government of Qatar to sell his Current TV to Al Jazeera America. Qatar is ruled by a combination of civil and sharia law. Sodomy is punishable by between one and three years in prison. Qatar is now cooperating with the Gulf Cooperative Countries to apply an anti-gay test to those who wish to immigrate to the country.**Bank of America.** Qatar currently holds a $1 billion stake in Bank of America.

Major Universities Including Harvard, Georgetown, Columbia, University of Arkansas and Berkeley. All these major universities have taken serious cash from the Saudi government. In 2005, Prince Alwaleed bin Tala Alsaud handed $20 million to Harvard and another $20 million to Georgetown. He stated, "Bridging the understanding between East and West is important for peace and tolerance." Georgetown President John J. DeGioia stated, "The gift will deepen Georgetown's ability to advance education in the fields of Islamic civilization and Muslim-Christian understanding, and strengthen its presence as a world leader in facilitating cross-cultural and inter-religious dialogue." Saudi Arabia punishes homosexuality with penalties ranging from death to lashings, from chemical castration to prison sentences.

Of course, former president Bill Clinton, in his lucrative speaking tours and continent-hopping, has spoken in the Gulf fiefdoms a number of times. And, oh, yes, the Abu Dhabi Investment Council owns most of that icon of American capitalism, the Chrysler Building – just for starters about what else the petro princes own in this country.

Daniel Greenfield on FrontPage ran an interesting and revealing post on May 6th about the gamboling and partying of the Sultan's gazillionaire offspring, "Will the Sultan of Brunei Stone His Gay Son to Death?"

Hollywood celebrities are protesting Brunei's adoption of Sharia Islamic law because it could mean gay men being stoned to death. Not to mention women. Also everyone from Christians to anyone who drinks a glass of beer could face cruel medieval punishments.

Brunei's ruling family, like those of most oil-rich nations, has been notorious for its party lifestyle. A member of the Sultan's harem has described violating his Sharia law together with the Sultan.

I could go on, but what would be the point? Whatever Azim's sexual preference is, does anyone believe that Islamic law would apply to him any more than it did to his uncle?

It's not just that Islamic law is evil, but that it doesn't apply to the elites who stone, whip and beat their people, but spend all their time partying.

<u>Vanity Fair</u> in July 2011, ran a piece by Mark Seal which explodes the pious, born-again-Muslim faith of the Sultan and his brother and offspring. Well, not so much the offspring.

For six weeks, starting last November 8, in the Supreme Court of the State of New York, in Manhattan, the two sides in a most unusual trial presented equally outlandish stories. The plaintiff, Prince Jefri Bolkiah, Brunei's notorious royal playboy, who has probably gone through more cash than any other human being on earth, tried to convince the jury that he was extremely naïve when it came to financial matters. He claimed that he never signed checks and that his business affairs had been managed entirely by four private secretaries and a coterie of advisers and attorneys, who ran his estimated 250 companies and all his other concerns.

By casting himself in that light, Prince Jefri, 56, hoped to make the jury believe that two of his own lawyers, Faith Zaman and Thomas Derbyshire, the attractive British husband-and-wife team sitting at the defense table, had ripped him off to the tune of a reported $23 million. This wasn't necessarily a bad strategy, because soon it seemed that only a simpleton would not have noticed the blatant chicanery he was accusing these attorneys of committing.

Imagine. And this is not a Sharia court, either, but an American law court. But the Sultan's sons, discussed by Greenfield above, are just as profligate, and this might be more in tune with Hollywood's newly-cast crowd of protesting extras. Mark Seal wrote about the Sultan and his brother:

Back home, the sultan erected a 1,788-room palace on 49 acres, "which is without equal in the world for offensive and ugly display," in the words of one British magnate, and celebrated his 50th birthday with a blowout featuring a concert by Michael Jackson, who was reportedly paid $17 million, in a stadium built for the occasion. (When the sultan flew in Whitney Houston for a performance, he is rumored to have given her a blank check and instructed her to fill it in for what she thought she was worth: more than $7 million, it turned out.) The brothers routinely traveled with 100-member entourages and emptied entire inventories of stores such as Armani and Versace, buying 100 suits of the same color at a time. When they partied, they indulged in just about everything forbidden in a Muslim country. Afforded four wives by Islamic law, they left their multiple spouses and scores of children in their palaces while they allegedly sent emissaries to comb the globe for the sexiest women they could find in order to create a harem the likes of which the world had never known.....

The Vanity Fair article contains much, much more detailed dirt on the Sultan and his family, but you'll need to read it yourselves.

So, what's the big deal about Sharia as practiced in Brunei? After all, Muslims practice it in every Western country named above, either formally, in lawsuits against "Islamophobic" critics or against communities that don't want mosques built anywhere near civilized people, or in impromptu applications of it, when they rape indigenous, non-Muslim women, establish no-go areas in Western cities, or demand that non-Muslims conform to their religious, dietary, and social practices.

Hollywood's notion of "social justice" relating to the Sultan of Brunei is very late in coming. And the telling thing about the protests is that the Sultan's imposition of Sharia in that pitiful country directly attacks Hollywood's own notorious "lifestyle." Suppose the Sultan had rounded up all the non-Muslims in Brunei, and had them executed? Would Hollywood turn out in its Birkenstocks and designer jeans to protest that?

Doubtful. If you're not a Muslim in Brunei and are persecuted, it's all your fault. After all, you can take "tolerance" too far.

May 2014

Religion vs. The Arts

A writer who presumes to champion "good" literature or "good" art but begins his essay with a supporting quotation from James Joyce is not someone I can regard seriously as a champion of anything. If any writer has helped to contribute to the destruction of literature, and, incidentally, of the other arts, it was James Joyce. See these descriptions of his *Ulysses* and *Finnegan's Wake*. Joyce's intellectual mentor was Immanuel Kant, a philosopher who strived to save religion from the Enlightenment. To wit:

> "I go to encounter for the millionth time the reality of experience and to forge in the smithy of my soul the uncreated conscience of my race." James Joyce, *Portrait of the Artist as a Young Man,* 1916

Whatever that means. I think it means that experience is "everything." But "experience" tells us nothing about what causes an experience.

Novelist and screenwriter Andrew Klavan doesn't enlighten us about what causes experiences in his February 7th FrontPage article, "The Trouble with the Arts," which is an excerpt from his pamphlet, "Crisis in the Arts: Why the Left owns the Culture and How Conservatives Can Begin to Take It Back." Klavan has assumed the role of the conservatives' doyen in shining armor to battle the artistic and political dragons of the Left. He has a war plan.

Klavan marshals two other supporting quotations, one from the poet Percy Bysshe Shelley ("Poets are the unacknowledged legislators of the world"), and one from the late conservative publicizer Andrew Breitbart ("Politics is downstream of culture").

Breitbart actually had the right thing in mind. He would seem to agree with novelist/philosopher Ayn Rand who wrote that politics would be the last thing to change in any nation's cultural renaissance. For a politics to change, a change in a nation's philosophy must occur first. America had a good start, with the ideas that caused a revolution. But those ideas were implicit and not explicit enough. The American Revolution was a consequence of men's revolt against secular and religious tyranny. But a nation can't sustain itself indefinitely on undefined ideas. The Founders were political philosophers, but for a nation's political philosophy to endure, it must be complemented and preceded by a specific view of man and existence. And that can be illustrated in art.

If its implicit philosophy is that man and reality are malleable and can be made to conform to a tyrant's or bureaucrat's wishes – a philosophy which governs the policies of the current occupant of the White House, one which actually began to be implemented long ago in the 19th century, we're only just now seeing its consequences and logical end – then whoever in the future occupies the White House must be raised in a culture whose philosophy is that man is a being of volitional consciousness and that reality is not an ephemeral, subjective figment of his imagination, but a rock-solid absolute that can't be evaded without incurring dire, life-threatening consequences.

The adage goes that you can't cheat an honest man. He can only sue for damages or a refund or laugh at the man who thinks he has cheated him. Reality, however, can't be cheated, either, and its retaliatory options are far more costly. Look at our society, our nation, today. "Reality," says Cyrus Skeen of the stock market crash of 1929 in *The Black Stone*, "has called in its markers."

I argue that quoting Joyce, a Catholic who regarded man as a Freudian monster governed by his bowel movements and as a beast unable to escape his inherent wickedness, insignificance, and corruption, was the correct choice for Klavan to quote. Klavan himself is a Christian convert and his article is rife with allusions and assertions that man must struggle against his alleged evil nature. He subscribes to the notion of Original Sin. Much of his fiction *oeuvre* is Christian in nature. It is of the "Left Behind" genre.

I would be amused by Klavan's presumptions if they didn't reflect on the real crisis, which, according to Klavan, is that if there is going to be a regeneration of American values and culture, it will be based on patriotism, family, and religion. But patriotism isn't enough to revive a love of country that clashes with what it is today. Patriotism is an emotion. Family and religion are not fundamental philosophies on which to ignite a renaissance. They are banal and so shop-worn that one can see right through them. "Family" is not a philosophic unit. Religion is merely a primitive form of philosophy that attempts to explain man and existence. Reviving it isn't going to solve any crisis in art. It didn't in the past, and won't in the future. Solving the energy "crisis" is not reinventing the horse or learning how to make candles.

Regarding a definition of art, Klavan first quotes Leo Tolstoy:

> "Art is a human activity consisting in this, that one man consciously, by means of certain external signs, hands on to others feelings he has lived through, and that other people are infected by these feelings and also experience them."
> Leo Tolstoy, *What is Art?*

He then builds on that role of "experience" and on Joyce's own rambling grunts about art:

> Art is a method of recording the ineffable inner experience of being human. There are no words that can directly describe what it is like to be self-consciously alive....
>
> So the purpose of art is not to edify or instruct, though it can instruct and often does edify. The purpose of art is not even to delight, though, if it's art, it will delight because that's its nature, that's the way it works. The purpose of art is to record and transmit the internal human experience.

Whose ineffable "internal human experience"? Klavan's? Yours? Your next-door neighbor's? Or is there a boilerplate, one-size-fits-all "human experience"? Klavan makes no distinction between the experiences of a Charles Manson and a Cyrano de Bergerac.

By way of contrast, here's a philosophical definition of art, together with a statement of its purpose, courtesy of Ayn Rand:

> Art is a selective re-creation of reality according to an artist's metaphysical value-judgments. Man's profound need of art lies in the fact that his cognitive faculty is conceptual, i.e., that he acquires knowledge by means of abstractions, and needs the power to bring his widest metaphysical abstractions into his immediate, perceptual awareness. Art fulfills this need: by means of a selective re-creation, it concretizes man's fundamental view of himself and of existence. It tells man, in effect, which aspects of his

202.

experience are to be regarded as essential, significant, important. In this sense, art teaches man how to use his consciousness. It conditions or stylizes man's consciousness by conveying to him a certain way of looking at existence.*

If your life depended on knowing the definition of art, whose definition would you count on? Rand's precise reduction of the term to its essentials, or Klavan's woozy flailing about in his gloppish "experiences" in the company of Tolstoy and Joyce in search of the "meaning of life"?

It's the difference between using a Colt Magnum .45 on a target and throwing pebbles at it.

What is a metaphysical value judgment? Is existence is to be valued, or feared? Is life is to be lived as an individual, or as a nameless, helpless cog in a collective? Does one live for oneself, or for the state, the collective, for the group? How men look at existence ultimately will determine what political system they choose to live under, or endure, or tolerate.

The secular version of Original Sin is that man is but a pitiful piece of protoplasm that ought to be controlled and regulated for the good of the greater protoplasm, and even extinguished, if necessary, if he gets too big for his state-mandated britches. Existence is a burden, say the secularist elites, and the state's purpose is to ameliorate the conditions of life by banishing its attributes and suppressing men who attempt to make living for anything but the state and the collective evil and punishable. The religious version of Original Sin is that individuals are born evil or contemptible or guilty of a wrong committed before they were even conceived.

Klavan has a foot in both versions.

> If the purpose of culture is to record and convey the internal human experience in its entirety, it is going to record and convey a good many things of which we disapprove. There is simply no getting around the wickedness, corruption, greed, lust and sheer troublemaking goofiness lodged in the hearts of the best of us — and therefore, there is no getting around their entertainment value or their legitimacy as subjects for art....

But while good and evil are real, the human heart is not in harmony with them and never has been. To paraphrase Saint Paul, we do not always do the good we want to do, and the evil we don't want to do, we keep on doing. Because we are fallen creatures then, there is, in human life, a price for every choice we make and a consequence for every action.

Klavan ironically chides some Christians for opposing what our culture has produced.

> Some evangelical Christians made the mistake of attacking the delightful Harry Potter novels because Potter is a wizard and wizardry and magic are against Christian teaching. But Potter's wizardry existed in a completely fantastical world that did not play by the same rules as the real world. In the context of *that* world, his fictional wizardry not only exemplified excellent moral values, it also laid the foundations for faith. The novels are deeply Christian when judged, not by their individual incidents, but by their overall effect. By condemning them, the evangelicals lost a hugely popular teaching tool.

One must wonder why evangelical Christians draw the line at Harry Potter's wizardry and the wizardry integral to Christian faith, i.e., the loaves and fishes, water into wine, rising from the dead, and other miracles.

Klavan cites numerous instances of his likes and dislikes in contemporary culture and the arts. But one of his dislikes stands out as a clue to his "humane" notion of what constitutes "bad" art:

> Conservatives are giddy with pleasure and relief when a popular novel or film doesn't thoroughly trash capitalism or sexual morality or faith in God. Meanwhile, the left wing writers of TV shows like *Law and Order* tear true stories from the headlines every single week and rewrite them to impose pro-left, anti-right values on their narratives. To cite but one example of many: in 2005, brain damaged Terri Schiavo was judicially starved to death at the request of her husband while evangelical Christian pro-life groups fought to save her. That same year, *Law and Order* produced a

204.

fictional version of the case in which an evangelical Christian engineered the murder of a Schiavo-like character's husband.

I *can* decide which is worse between a left-wing rewrite of the <u>Terry Schiavo</u> case that demonizes Christian evangelicals, and Klavan's complaint which defends evangelical Christians who fought to save the life of an individual whose body is alive but whose capacity for thought, values, and independence were gone. The *Law and Order* episode was just another naturalistic, hackneyed screed created by mediocrities, and comes a literal dime-a-dozen on modern television. Would Klavan have wanted Terry Shiavo to remain alive? Would there have been such a person as Terry Shiavo inside the body? Or any person at all? Klavan doesn't say. But his outrage over how the leftist writers portrayed the evangelical Christians should serve as a clue.

Then there is Klavan's penchant for what could only be called "hard-boiled religious naturalism" and how the left-wing critical establishment treats it.

> And, of course, when Mel Gibson's beautiful *The Passion of the Christ* ignited a wave of faith-based excitement among evangelicals… well, what happened to Jesus in that movie was nothing compared to what left wing critics did to Mel!

Anyone who has seen Mel Gibson's opus will concede that it is one of the most gruesome depictions of the Crucifixion every filmed, and unnecessarily gruesome even for a religious film. Yet, Klavan calls it "beautiful."

Because Klavan eschews the role of philosophy, his campaign to combat the left-wing artistic establishment in Hollywood, the publishing industry, and the "social media," his efforts will come to naught. It will not be "reclaimed" by conservatives in the current philosophical climate, not next year, not in twenty years.

> The vision that inspired the American experiment in liberty was a vision created and preserved and handed down through works of western art and culture. It was a complex vision of man as a flawed creature in a moral universe striving toward the freedom for which he was made…. Uncensored, that voice, intentionally or not, consciously or

not, will always cry out for the very things conservatives most believe in: personal independence and lasting love, a good life today and a better life tomorrow, faith in a God who is no stranger to our suffering and who will yet become the father of our joy.

Conservatives, however, are consummate altruists, and it is altruism that is responsible for the cultural miasma Klavan excoriates. Conservatism shares the same deadly premises of altruism with the statists, the socialists, and every tyranny that has ever existed.

On the other hand, Klavan would do well to heed Ayn Rand's fundamental prescription for cultural renewal and "taking back" the country's purpose and spirit:

> As in the case of an individual, so in the case of a culture; disasters can be accomplished subconsciously, but a cure cannot. A cure in both cases requires conscious knowledge, i.e., a consciously grasped, explicit philosophy.

> It is impossible to predict the time of a philosophical Renaissance. One can only define the road to follow, not its length. What is certain, however, is that every aspect of Western culture needs a new code of ethics – a *rational ethics* – as a precondition of rebirth. And, perhaps, no aspect needs it more desperately than the realm of art.

> When reason and philosophy are reborn, literature will be the first phoenix to rise out of today's ashes. And, armed with a code of rational values, aware of its own nature, confident of the supreme importance of its mission, Romanticism will have come of age.**

Some of the most magnificent art of the past had religious themes or themes derived from religion (e.g., Michelangelo's heroic "David," the somber "Pieta," and the Sistine Chapel). The subject of that art was man himself, with religion serving as an excuse to portray him. Romanticism will have come of age when men no longer need an excuse to portray him as the heroic being he has been, is today, and can always be, *sans* supernatural excuses.

*"Art and Cognition," (1971) p. 45. *The Romantic Manifesto: A Philosophy of Literature*. New York: Signet, 1971. Second Revised Edition, 1975.
**"What is Romanticism?" p. 122. Op. cit. 1969

February 2014

§   The End   §

Other Titles in This Series

- *Running Out My Guns: Broadsides in the War of Ideas*
- *Broadsides in the War of Ideas*
- *Corsairs & Freebooters*
- *Boarding Parties & Grappling Hooks*
- *Letters of Marque*

Fiction: Published from Perfect Crime Books

- *With Distinction*
- *First Prize*
- *Presence of Mind*
- *Honors Due*

Fiction: Published from Patrick Henry Press

- *Whisper the Guns*
- *We Three Kings*
- *Run From Judgment*
- *China Basin*
- *The Head of Athena*
- *The Daedâlus Conspiracy*
- *The Chameleon*
- *A Crimson Overture*
- *The Black Stone*

Historical Fiction from Patrick Henry Press

- ➢ *Sparrowhawk: Jack Frake*

- ➢ *Sparrow hawk: Hugh Kenrick*

- ➢ *Sparrowhawk: Caxton*

- ➢ *Sparrowhawk: Empire*

- ➢ *Sparrowhawk: Revolution*

- ➢ *Sparrowhawk: War*

- ➢ *The New Sparrowhawk Companion*

www.ingramcontent.com/pod-product-compliance
Lightning Source LLC
Chambersburg PA
CBHW070108290526
45789CB00005B/1961